Praise for *What Animals Teach Us*

"*What Animals Teach Us*, with equal parts wisdom, wit, and warmth, describes the special connection and showcases the virtuous characteristics of animals that, frankly, most humans can only strive for. An outstanding and unforgettable celebration of the special friendship of animals."

—MARTY BECKER, D.V.M., veterinary contributor for
"Good Morning America" and coauthor of
Chicken Soup for the Pet Lover's Soul and
Chicken Soup for the Cat & Dog Lover's Soul

"Thank you for celebrating how much we learn from the animals we love!"

—BETTY WHITE, actress, author,
and animal advocate

"Reading *What Animals Teach Us* is the next best thing to sharing your life with an animal companion. Numerous stories of loyalty, trust, respect, compassion, and love fill its pages and they will fill your heart. This inspirational book will change your life and the lives of the animals with whom we share this planet. Read it, be mindful, and be sure to play more . . . and more."

—MARC BEKOFF, professor of biology,
University of Colorado at Boulder, and author of
Strolling With Our Kin and coauthor of *Nature's Life Lessons*

"This wonderful book chronicles how hard and well our pets are working to teach us lifesaving lessons about love."

—MARGARET WHEATLEY, author of
Leadership and the New Science

"*What Animals Teach Us* is like bathing in the sounds of a beautifully harmonized symphony. Mary Hessler-Key has blended wonderfully told stories of animals' spiritual qualities with inspiring and practical applications to humans' daily lives. She teaches us what animals have taught her, and we're all enriched by the lessons."

—ALLEN AND LINDA ANDERSON,
authors of *Angel Animals*

"Mary Hessler-Key blends storytelling and science into an extremely readable book. This book not only clarifies the lessons we learn from our pets but coaches us on how to apply them in our own lives. It pointed out for me, once again, how admirably high of a standard dogs and cats set for us. Prepare to be both moved and motivated!"

—JOYCE BRIGGS, executive director of
PETsMART Charities

"Mary Hessler-Key has given a practical and popular voice to the potency of the 'interbeing' of all things. These lessons are the very best kind of magic—useful and powerful."

—BOB ALLEN, CEO, Integrity Arts and Technology Inc.

"Mary Hessler-Key's poignant stories, combined with reliable data, illustrate the importance of animals in fostering a humane society. We will be using this book as a guide in our educational outreach programs."

—CAROLE LEWIS, founder,
WildLife on Easy Street, a nonprofit cat sanctuary

In order to create the best future, we all need to learn to appreciate diversity and what we can learn from creatures different from us. Mary Hessler-Key uniquely outlines life lessons from our animal companions that we can incorporate daily. Fabulous!

—PATRICIA ABURDENE,
coauthor of Megatrends for Women

WHAT ANIMALS TEACH US

LOVE, LOYALTY, HEROISM,

AND OTHER LIFE LESSONS

FROM OUR PETS

MARY HESSLER-KEY, PH.D.

Prima Publishing

Published by Prima Publishing, Roseville, California. Member of the Crown Publishing Group, a division of Random House, Inc.

Random House, Inc. New York, Toronto, London, Sydney, Auckland

PRIMA PUBLISHING and colophon are trademarks of Random House, Inc., registered with the United States Patent and Trademark Office.

Library of Congress Cataloging-in-Publication Data
Hessler-Key, Mary.
    What animals teach us : love, loyalty, heroism, and other life lessons from our pets / Mary Hessler-Key.
       p.   cm.
    Includes bibliographical references and index.
    ISBN 0-7615-3607-8
    1. Pets—Psychological aspects. 2. Pets—Social aspects. 3. Pet owners—Psychology. 4. Human-animal relationships. I. Title.
SF411.47.H47   2001
636.088'7'019—dc21   2001052098

01 02 03 04 HH 10 9 8 7 6 5 4 3 2 1
Printed in the United States of America

First Edition

Visit us online at www.primapublishing.com

To my husband, Lewis,
and our furry family of cats:
Jasper, Sheba, and Groucho

And to my grandmother, Eva;
my mother, Helen;
and my sister, Joan,
for their loving support of me over the years.

CONTENTS

FOREWORD

WE LIVE in a complicated world, often far removed from the natural world. Some people are fortunate enough to live in the countryside where they can see the cycles of life right in their own backyards. For most of us, however, the only link to the mysterious world of nature is the family pet.

In the days when most people worked the land, animals were not only our daily companions; they were also part of the working team. Horses were our transportation and helped us till the fields. Dogs helped round up the cattle or the sheep and guarded the homestead. Cats kept the mouse and rat populations down. Today, most cats and dogs do little of that kind of work, but they are invaluable to us, providing an intimate connection to the natural world that most of us have lost contact with.

In *What Animals Teach Us*, Mary Hessler-Key shows us how the animals who share our homes can teach us valuable lessons to take us through life.

As sanctuary director of Best Friends Animal Sanctuary, I have crossed paths with many kinds of animals, and each one of them has shown me something important about myself or taught me something priceless about the magical world they live in. For example, Fenris, an Australian shepherd mix, came to Best Friends after being badly shot in his back leg. I surmised he was very old because of his general physical condition. To make matters worse, his leg injury was deeply infected. I didn't think he would be with us for long, so I set about making his last days the best I could.

With good vet care, however, Fenris was able to keep his leg. And with a nutritious diet and lots of love, the years just peeled away from him until I realized that he was in fact a young dog who had aged prematurely because of severe neglect. He taught me never to give up and to keep all my options open.

Fenris had every right to be a bitter, angry dog after what had happened to him, but he wasn't. He was always loving, always patient, and always present. We became very close, and until he passed away at a ripe old age, he was a constant reminder of the indomitable spirit of dogs.

While dogs and cats are the most common companion animals, it's important to remember that animal "teachers" come in many different forms. During a period of time when I was very depressed about a failed enterprise, my angels came in the form of chickens—a species of the animal kingdom not generally known for intelligence. My chickens, however, all knew how to be the best chickens they could be. I remember many days when I was feeling down and sitting by their coop. I'd watch them interact with each other and go about their daily business. Their simple approach to life brought me back in touch with the present. By following their lead and striving for a life of simplicity, I was able to identify what was truly important to me. I learned how fulfilling life could be when you accept yourself for who you are, warts and all.

Love is often in short supply in our busy, frantic lives. Fortunately, our animals are a constant reminder that loving takes so little time and can be communicated effortlessly by a wet nose nudging our elbow or a soft purr as we catch our breath before going on to the next task. In this book we learn the real priorities—like how loving and being loved by our animals changes our lives.

This book has something for people of all ages. For example, many children learn about death for the first time through the loss of a family pet. Mary shows how the passing of a pet can help young people come to terms with this inevitability.

She also shows us the tremendous role animals can play in the lives of seniors, providing an unspoken comfort and physical contact with a living being. Mary shares wonderful stories about older folks gripped by illnesses of aging who are able to maintain a true connection with a beloved pet even as the rest of their world fades away in lost memories.

Animals are our greatest teachers because they show us how to be true to ourselves. They never lie or pretend to be something they are not. They teach us simplicity in our complicated lives, helping us stay in touch with our inner selves, our true instincts, and our own healing power.

I hope that reading this book and applying its principles will make you feel good about yourself and that you'll be encouraged to make the world a better place for all the creatures with whom we share it.

Faith Maloney
Best Friends Animal Sanctuary
Kanab, Utah

ACKNOWLEDGMENTS

I WANT TO acknowledge all of you who have shared your wonderful animal stories with me. Your willingness to take the time to add to all our learning means so much. As I wrote this book, St. Francis of Assisi's love for animals influenced me daily. His example touches my heart, and he serves as a role model for me.

A special thank you to my very talented editor and coach, Dawn Josephson, who has consistently inspired me to write better; to Chris Wholeben, business manager of Mary Key & Associates, who assisted and supported me throughout the writing of this book; and to Dawn Jones and John Davies for their help and responsiveness.

To my loving friends who took the time to help by finding stories, reading drafts of chapters, and most of all, in supporting me: Catherine Karlak, Carol Maier, Katy Mims, Howard Baskin, Kathryn Mason, Kate Steichen, Randy Sights, Kelly Lynn Pipkin, Sarah Jordan-Holmes, Jan Baskin, Merci Lopez, Tekla Ulrich, Elli Sorenson, and Anne Thal.

Without my husband, Lewis's, support and his willingness to take care of things at home, I would not have been able to complete the book on time. Thank you, my darling, for who you are.

In researching this book, several people took time from their busy schedules to generously offer their professional expertise so that the lessons and research represent the current thinking on the topic: Dr. Eddie Garcia, Faith Maloney of Best Friends Animal Sanctuary, Carole Lewis of Save the Cats, Dr. Marc Bekoff, Dr. Randy Lange, Dr. Marty Becker, and Linda Anderson of Angel Animals.

I so appreciate the help from Prima Publishing, especially from Denise Sternad and Michelle McCormack, who guided me along the way.

INTRODUCTION

A NIMALS HAVE always been part of my life experiences. While I was growing up, my cat Cookie was my constant companion. No matter what happened, Cookie was always there to laugh with, sing to, and cry with. Cookie helped me deal with the complexities of the adult world by allowing me to be myself in any situation. He was patient and would listen to my deepest secrets. A "latch-key kid," I looked forward to Cookie always being there to greet me when I came home from school.

My childhood friends had companion animals, too. I loved going over to their houses and playing with their dogs, horses, birds, hamsters, and turtles. I found being in the presence of animals freeing, as they interacted so openly and lovingly with others and me. Most animals I've met, especially Cookie, taught me more about how to be a friend to others.

Throughout my life, I've always been fascinated with learning and with how we humans grow and develop. Like many children, I started asking "Why?" about everything. But instead of getting over it, I became more absorbed with wanting to know why. In college I studied human development, psychology, learning theory, and business. The common theme throughout this course of study was: How do we as humans grow and be all we can be while here on earth?

Upon graduating, I was immediately attracted to the world of consulting because it gave me an observer's view to the inner workings of the human mind and spirit at work. I was intrigued with how corporate cultures formed and how they could foster transformation and growth. As I consulted with businesses around the world, I saw how diverse people have similar goals, like finding meaning in their work, providing for the future, and being part of something bigger than themselves. Working with such a varied group of individuals and learning from their experiences gave me the opportunity to rethink my life's plan.

After six years of consulting, I, too, wanted to be part of a bigger cause. I left the security of a large consulting firm to be part of a start-up venture that offered me the chance to improve women's health care. One year later, my dream of growing a company that had a compelling mission was dashed when government regulations made operating the business impossible. Without a job and feeling scared, I depended on my cats, Sheba and Jasper, to give me the support I needed. They taught me to stay in the present and to cherish each day. Because I was at home, I had the pleasure of observing them more closely and more often. Their love and approach to life inspired me to write my first book, *The Entrepreneurial Cat: Thirteen Ways to Transform Your Work Life.* That's when I became an entrepreneur.

When I went to book signings, I would sometimes take Jasper, or Jazzie as I call him, with me. When Jazzie couldn't accompany me, I would bring cats from a local shelter in hopes that someone at the bookstore would want to adopt them. I noticed that when people approached me, they seemed to relax, and they enjoyed visiting with the cats. That's when I began to hear people's animal stories, wonderful true tales about how companion animals enriched their lives. Some of those are included in this book.

Over the years, the animals in my life have taught me that love, acceptance, and celebrating differences are all part of personal transformation. We experience being part of a greater whole when we realize the boundaries that seem to separate us are really an illusion. But we humans seek our own identity, and the self-absorption can cause us to forget our interconnectedness with plants, animals, and each other. And that closes us off to the teachings of other species.

This book is written to raise the consciousness of humans about the contribution our companion animals make to our learning and growth. It goes over many important "pet lessons," which are life lessons that animals teach us. Through animals, we can learn about unconditional love, loyalty, life cycles, following our instincts, healing, grieving, playing, and heroism. Just like me, many of you have stories about companion animals that have brought tremendous value to your lives. Each chapter in this book introduces a life lesson we can learn from our animal companions, shows real-life examples of our animal companions' actions, presents the latest research to support the premise that we can learn these different lessons from our pets, and ends with some Pet Lessons exercises to help you apply to your daily life what you learn from companion animals.

I'm interested in your feedback on this book and in your stories. Please take the time to share those with me. And I know many of you reading this book work tirelessly for the animals—thank you for all you do!

Mary Hessler-Key
mary@maryhesslerkey.com

WHAT ANIMALS
TEACH US

CHAPTER ONE

Lessons of Unconditional Love and Friendship

"In loving Flora (my cat), I knew I would find a way to love myself as well."

—SUSAN CHERNAK McELROY

TRUE POWER comes from loving unconditionally. Our churches tell us this, proponents of psychological health advocate it, and, although it's couched in a mixed message, our society instructs us to love others as we would love ourselves. Yet for some reason, it is very difficult for us to give unconditional love to a fellow human.

That's why it is so remarkable that we give unconditional love so freely and easily to animals. Without uttering a word, animals have the innate—and uncanny—ability to release our capacity to love unconditionally. We humans trust our companion animals, from beloved family pets to rescued strays. We trust these furry creatures so much that we are able let down our guards with them and love them unconditionally, as they so freely love us.

Through our connection with companion animals we can grow spiritually, for it is often through an animal's love for us that we learn to love ourselves just as we are. Companion animals' unconditional acceptance of us as their friends opens a window through which we can see ourselves in a gentler and more compassionate light. As children, many of us sought the solace of our family dogs or cats when our peers called us names. We knew our furry friends would offer us love and acceptance no matter what. As adults, we know that the cold wet nose nuzzling us and the feathered wings brushing up against us could care less if we don't put on our makeup or don't shave or if we have a studio apartment instead of a five-bedroom home with a three-car garage and a sunroom for their basking.

From our companion animals, we can learn many "pet lessons," my term for the life lessons pets offer purely through the example of their own behavior. Unconditional love, for ourselves and for others, is one of the most profound of these pet lessons. Through our friendships with our companion animals, we discover the essential lesson: that we are all connected through love.

A Second Chance at Love

George's eyes glaze over when he talks about Deacon, or Deke, as he was affectionately known. Deke was a fuzzy black terrier with round, loving eyes and a knack for warming hearts. He was George's best friend for 12 years. Over those twelve years, George and Deke grew into many routines, patterns of behavior that became second nature to them. These routines helped to keep them close, both physically and emotionally.

George has his own painting business and has customers as far away as 50 miles. He prefers to get an early start, so he sets his alarm clock. But Deke always did the alarm one better. Every morning, no matter what, Deke beat George's alarm clock by five minutes for a dose of nuzzling to start the day. Then Deke waited outside the bathroom door while George showered. Every once in a while Deke might let out a little whimper just to say, "I'm still here." But other than that, he waited—patiently and quietly. Once the waiting was over, he would spring excitedly to his feet, and he and George would head to the kitchen for their breakfast. Every night, Deke snuggled up to George for about a half hour as if to say, "I just need a little affection." Once he got his nightly dose, he was satisfied with sleeping at George's feet.

Though the routines George shared with Deke became standard practice, George never took them for granted. In fact, his friendship with Deke sustained George through some hard times. George felt lonely during some of these trials. When he and his wife, Julie, were having some problems with their marriage, he would sometimes feel uneasy just thinking about coming home. But every night, rain or shine, dark or light, Deke was in the carport, waiting for George to come home.

During dinner, if Julie had made steak—not one of George's favorites—George would sneak some to Deke when Julie wasn't looking—and Deke was good at keeping this little secret of theirs. After dinner, George always took Deke for his nightly walk. This gave George the chance to unwind and to think, and though he didn't necessarily speak aloud to Deke, George just knew that Deke understood his thoughts . . . his emotions.

One day George noticed that Deke was moving a little slower than usual and was very lethargic. He didn't seem as enthusiastic about going for a walk, and he didn't want to play. Julie mentioned that she had noticed that Deke was sleeping more during the day while George was at work. It was obvious that Deke simply wasn't himself, and they both felt that Deke needed to get checked out by the vet ahead of his annual exam. After an initial exam, the vet wanted to immediately run some tests and proceed with whatever medical procedures might be necessary. George felt a burning in his heart. Just as Deke could sense when George was struggling with a problem, George knew right away that Deke was going through more than a minor ailment. Though he didn't want to think the worst, an underlying flow of fear was racing through him.

The vet called to let George know that the tests "weren't good." George asked, "What do you mean? What's wrong?" The doctor explained that abnormalities were showing up in the blood work, the x rays, and the physical exam, but he didn't want to make a final diagnosis without more information. The doctor scheduled exploratory surgery for the following morning, and Deke spent the night at the clinic.

That night it was rainy and cold, and the wind was howling. George and Julie had a fire going as they sat together in the living room reading the newspaper. George was having a hard time concentrating. Suddenly, the fierce wind blew the unlocked front door open and thrust a small dark animal right into the living room. At first George thought it was a rat, but it turned out to be a young black cat, a female. Her black fur was soaking wet from the downpour.

George and Julie approached the frightened animal, talking to her gently, telling her not to be scared. Their calming voices eased her, and she let them dry her off as best they could. They fed the young cat some leftover meatloaf and milk. After dinner, she seemed so content by the fire that neither George nor Julie had the heart to put her back out in the storm, and they were both enjoying the presence of an animal on that difficult night. They missed Deke so much—the cat somehow helped them feel closer to him.

The next morning, about five minutes before the alarm was going to go off, the cat jumped up on George and Julie's bed and began to lick George's hand. Then the new friend waited outside the bathroom while George showered, but he was so preoccupied with Deke that he didn't take much note of it.

When the phone rang later that morning, George leapt to answer it, hoping it was the vet. It was. As the doctor calmly explained that surgery had revealed Deke's body was filled with cancer, George doubled over. The doctor advised euthanizing Deke, and although George knew the doctor's advice made sense, that it was what was best for Deke, it was the hardest decision George had ever had to make. He didn't work that day, and he and Julie went together to the vet's office to say good-bye to their close friend. That night they cried as they looked at pictures of Deke and reminisced about their beloved dog.

Before they retired for bed that night, the black cat nuzzled with George for about 30 minutes, then slept at George's feet. The next morning she again waited patiently outside his shower. George shook his head and thought he must be imagining this coincidence.

George found it incredibly difficult to work that day. Flashes of Deke distracted him as he somberly painted a newly renovated stucco house. He caught himself tearing up at memories of his faithful friend. As he went through the day, George felt as if Deke's smiling brown eyes were following him. He longed to pet his loving pal one more time and feel the texture of his black fur between his fingers. "Deke is gone, and I won't see him again," George had to keep reminding himself. He sobbed all the way home.

That evening, George returned home later than usual. His continual thoughts of Deke had made the job go slower, so he had to stay later to finish. And the thought of pulling up into the driveway and not seeing Deke made his heart ache even more. When George drove up, however, he was amazed to see the black cat sitting there in the carport, right on Deke's spot. Julie served steak that night, and the cat and George shared it.

"This is incredible!" George exclaimed. "Who is this animal?" George and Julie named the cat Spanky. And for ten years now, Spanky has continued to perform these and other rituals that were George and Deke's.

When asked what he learned from this, George said, "I got in touch with God again. First, I learned that Deke loved me unconditionally and he was always there for me. Having Spanky enter our lives was like God and Deke got together to make sure I continued to love and open myself up. The miracle of it all changed my life—and Julie's, too."

This pet lesson would seem unlikely were it not absolutely true. George's dog helped him to love himself more, and the miracle of Spanky's presence continues to teach George about love. And George and Julie both feel that they are closer today because of their pets' devotion and unconditional love.

The Human–Pet Connection

THE HUMAN–ANIMAL BOND is powerful. The latest survey from the American Pet Products Manufacturers Association found that about 59 percent of American households have some kind of pet.[1] In a study of 122 families with companion animals published in the *Journal of Mental Health Counseling*, almost a third of the subjects reported that they felt closer to their dog than to any other family member.[2] Clearly, pets are an essential part of the family unit.

In his book, *The Unbearable Lightness of Being*, Milan Kundera points out that the love between pets and humans is unconditional and completely selfless.[3] People don't try to make a companion animal over in their own image. We don't say, "If she would just be witty at dinner parties, I could love her." We don't wonder, "Do I love him more than he loves me?"

Animals are a link to happiness and understanding. Our companion animals don't know hate or jealousy or spite. They don't care about fat versus skinny, rich versus poor. They accept us for who we really are—imperfections, limitations, and all—and being with companion animals satisfies our need for intimacy, our need to nurture, and our need to be in touch with nature. Most of all, it fulfills our human desire to be in the presence of a living creature who loves us without stipulations. For all these reasons and more, the love and friendship between our companion animals and us plays an important role in our well-being.

Boris Levinson, an American child psychiatrist, has conducted some of the more notable research regarding the human-pet relationship.[4] Levinson believed that pets could directly enhance people's emotional development by being constant sources of companionship, comfort, and security during periods of alienation, rejection, or crisis. He believed that this capacity to offer unconditional affection and support was the key to both the strength and the importance of the human-animal relationship.

Among the first to put Levinson's theories to the test was a husband-and-wife psychiatric team at Ohio State University, Sam and Elizabeth Corson. The doctors selected 50 withdrawn and uncommunicative patients and allowed them to choose a particular dog to interact with.[5] By the end of the study, three patients had withdrawn from participation. According to the Corsons, the companion animals helped the remaining 47 participants develop self-respect, independence, and self-confidence. The pets acted as a social catalyst, forging positive links between the patient and others, thus creating a widening circle of warmth and approval. The Corsons believed the dogs induced these changes by providing patients with a special kind of nonthreatening, nonjudgmental affection.[6]

To better understand how the human-animal bond develops and the sheer strength of it, consider for a moment how quickly a bond can spring up between companion animals and humans. When we get a new puppy, kitten, bird, or hamster, we often feel an immediate intimacy. Many people reveal that they kiss, hug, and cuddle their new pet at the first meeting. Unlike the bond between humans, the human-animal bond requires very little courting, no "getting to know you" phase. We have an immediate base of trust that allows us to communicate with our companion animal on a nonverbal level. Since there's no need to impress the animal, we instinctively let our guard down and form an immediate and long-lasting bond with them. Often, no matter what happens from that day on, the bond never diminishes; it only grows stronger.

Love at First Sight

Skeezers was Kathryn's best friend. Kathryn had adopted the longhaired, gray-and-white, tiger-striped cat from a friend who was moving to another state. Skeezers would not be everyone's first choice: She weighed in at 18 pounds and had long fur that made her look even larger. She purred constantly, which some people found annoying. Yet when Kathryn first saw her, it was "love at first sight." Skeezers's size didn't faze her—her initial instinct was to reach out and touch this gentle giant of a cat. And she saw Skeezers's snoring as part of the cat's charm.

Kathryn, single, a customer relations professional, had lived with several cats over the years, but Skeezers was the one that taught her the most about unconditional love. With Skeezers, she learned just how deep that love could be and how much affection one cat can offer.

When Kathryn would come home from a hard day at work, Skeezers would greet her at the door. Skeezers would brush up against Kathryn's leg and purr, as if to say, "Welcome back. I've missed you." With Skeezers's generous outpouring of love, Kathryn couldn't help but reciprocate. Kathryn and Skeezers would often snuggle up on the peach-colored living room couch as Kathryn watched a movie or read the newspaper. And Skeezers was not discriminating with her affection. All who visited the house received a display of affection and enthusiasm. The pet lesson Kathryn learned from this is how important it is to make everyone feel welcome in her life.

Kathryn's position in customer relations often left her feeling as if she had nothing left to give outside of work. She would routinely come home stressed and worn-out, feeling alone and drained. Like a lot of us, she sometimes felt that her job was thankless, that her efforts at work weren't always appreciated. But after cuddling with Skeezers for a few moments or watching the cat roll on the floor in pleasure at having her home, she would quickly perk up. Her cat's displays of love and enthusiasm would soon have her asking herself, "Why am I holding on to this tenseness and irritability after I leave the office?" Her cat's playful antics and desire to lighten her mood taught her the importance of companionship and loving others. She soon found that her daily problems were bearable as long as she kept the same positive perspective her cat always showed the world.

Kathryn strove to imitate her cat's approach to life. Skeezers was a cheerful, upbeat companion who never fussed or showed displeasure at anything, except when she was getting a bath. Skeezers's pleasant personality helped Kathryn realize that each day should be enjoyed as if it were her last. Living this way has made her a better friend to both animals and people. It has also made her more appreciative of the inherent gifts each creature on earth has to offer.

Through caring for Skeezers, Kathryn understood how hung up the human psyche can get on the little things that really don't matter. Her cat's unconditional love helped her let go of the trivial matters that she would routinely dwell on, such as getting cut off in traffic or encountering a rude person at work. Her cat's ultimate message was to focus on what is really important in life, namely to love and be loved.

Skeezers died on June 2 because of kidney failure. Although she is gone, Skeezers is still a big part of Kathryn's life. Whenever she feels weary, down, or in need of a friend, Kathryn pictures Skeezers curled up beside her and gains strength from her memory. "Skeezers ultimately taught me that unconditional love can make a big impact on the lives of others," Kathryn asserts. "It's a lesson that I strive to share with those I come in contact with."

The Companionship Factor

THE COMPANIONSHIP that pets offer is often the number one reason for their presence in the family. In fact, in one study conducted by *Psychology Today*, 80 percent of the pet owners surveyed revealed that they receive more companionship from their animals than from friends and neighbors and that their pets are equal to family members and relatives in importance.[7] Even more remarkable, in the majority of surveys about pet ownership that have been conducted, most respondents have given "companionship" or "friendship" as their principal reason for keeping a companion animal.[8]

James Serpell, author of *In the Company of Animals*, believes that companion animals have the capacity to "reconnect people with the outside world by breaking down the vicious circle of nonverbal misunderstandings that surrounds them."[9] He goes on to say that companion animals may be providing people with a special kind of emotional support that relationships between people often lack.

Breaking Down Emotional Walls

Tom always felt that he would be the last person on earth to have a dog. Tom grew up in Queens, New York, and his wife, Jean, grew up in Brooklyn. Because of their city lifestyle, neither of them ever had a pet while growing up. The tall skyscrapers and crowded apartments left little room for an animal of any kind. Even as adults, pets were never a part of the picture because of their hectic schedules—their focus was on their careers, then careers plus raising their children. There were always business deals to negotiate, meetings to conduct, and school plays to attend.

At the time a pet came into their lives, Tom and Jean were owners of a direct marketing business. Tom's determination to succeed precluded his interest in anything else and had earned him the reputation of being ruthless. Tom had been poor as a youngster, and his family didn't have a lot of resources. He grew up envying those who had money, and as he got older, he became more and more determined to succeed. As head of the company, Tom would stop at nothing to get his way. If he didn't get what he wanted, he'd be "in your face." He often reprimanded subordinates and was very Machiavellian in his approach toward people in order to get what he wanted. For most of his life, he had no spirituality, no business morals, and few ethics. His philosophy was to do whatever it took to be successful, at almost any cost.

An enthusiastic and energetic 12 pounds of unconditional love, Tara, was destined to change Tom's life. Tara was a black peek-a-poo ("peek" for Pekinese and "poo" for poodle). Tom's youngest daughter, Lisa, gave Tara to him on his 49th birthday. But she knew her father, and she was smart enough to add a qualification: "Dad," she said, "this is your birthday present, but if you decide you don't want to keep Tara, I will." Walking, grooming, and feeding a dog seemed like it would be too much of an intrusion to his bottom-line-oriented life, but, after giving it some thought, Tom decided to try life with a pet on a one-day-at-a-time basis.

During the next few months, a transformation occurred. Jean began noticing changes in Tom. She was astounded one day when Tom didn't overreact to a mistake a staff member made that resulted in a customer taking business elsewhere. She watched as Tom (with Tara in his lap), calmly questioned the employee about what happened, and offered ways to correct the error in the future. He never raised his voice, surprising everyone in the office, including himself.

That was the day Tom noticed that he had changed. Looking back, Tom realized that Tara's presence softened his heart and that she made him feel a new kind of love—one that was unselfish and unconditional. Tom felt that Tara, who would often lie across his feet, could sense his energy level and read his moods. One time when Tom was very sick with the flu, Tara lay at his side day and night, nuzzling him and licking his burning cheek with soothing wet kisses. She wouldn't even eat unless allowed to eat by his bed.

The more Tom experienced Tara's unconditional love, the more sensitive he became toward people and animals. "Thanks to Tara, I opened my heart to God again," says Tom. "I find myself wanting to thank God for her presence. Not since I was an altar boy did I feel any spirituality in my life." As a result of Tara's love, Tom started praying again and connecting with other people in the spiritual community. He asserts that Tara's love helped him discover a whole new dimension to his life. Her unconditional love and acceptance taught Tom the importance of love and caring for others.

Today, Tom and Jean have six dogs, two cats, and two miniature donkeys. They routinely adopt older dogs who don't have a home. Rather than visions of financial gain, Tom is dreaming of opening a convalescent home for aging dogs. Both he and Jean believe that aging dogs have so much to give and are often overlooked by those seeking loyal companions.

Tara has passed on, but Tom and Jean have kept her memory alive by donating a run at Best Friends Animal

Sanctuary. "Tara's Run" is a roofed enclosure that gives dogs at Best Friends more space for exercise and training sessions. It also serves as a get-acquainted area for people and dogs to do just that when they're thinking about adopting each other.

~~~~~~~~

Endless Love

All her life, Fran wanted to be a mom. As a child, she played endlessly with her baby dolls, dressing them up and carting them around in their strollers as if they were living, breathing babies. Throughout her teen years and into her 20s, the image of herself as a mom didn't waver. She dated throughout her 20s, but "Mr. Right"—the man with whom she wanted to spend the rest of her life and have a family— was nowhere in sight.

Then, shortly after turning 30, Fran met Dennis. She immediately fell for his warm personality and his sparkling blue eyes. She welcomed his sincerity and sense of humor into her life. In Dennis's arms, Fran felt safe and loved. And the two had much in common—they both enjoyed the outdoors, cycling, good Italian food, and working out. Fran and Dennis soon fell in love and talked of marriage.

Despite all their similarities, the couple had one important difference. Dennis, who was ten years older than Fran, had been married before and had a son, Brett, from that marriage. When the two began talking of raising a family of their own, Dennis expressed a lot of doubt about having more children. Even though he loved Fran dearly and wanted to do everything possible to make her happy, he did not want to become a parent again.

Fran had an important decision to make. She could stay with the man she loved even though it would probably mean she would never fulfill her lifelong dream of becoming a mom, or she could end their relationship and continue her search. Because she loved Dennis so much, she decided to marry him without resolving the issue of whether to have children. Luckily, as the marriage progressed, the two were so happy with their life together that they ultimately decided not to pursue having a family together. Fran was content being Brett's stepmom, and she didn't want a baby or anything else to disrupt the new family they had formed. They had a routine in their lives that worked for them.

On Christmas Eve 1998, however, everything changed. Fran went to the gym, and Dennis took a long run. About a half mile from the gym, Dennis noticed a small black dog that was obviously lost. Still a puppy growing into his feet and his tail, he looked like a combination of black Lab and Doberman. The puppy had no collar, and he was obviously cold and hungry as he stood there shivering in the cold afternoon. The desperate look in his eyes begged Dennis to help him.

Dennis stopped, and the dog immediately came to him. As Dennis began to walk, the dog followed, and by the time he got to the gym, he and this black dog with the loving eyes had bonded. Dennis knocked on the gym's glass window to get Fran's attention. When she noticed him outside knocking, she walked over to where he was. Dennis then held the dog up so Fran could see. When she saw her husband's new companion, she came running out.

"Who is this?" was Fran's first question. Dennis explained how he met the dog and said that he wanted to keep it. Fran was against the idea. They had decided not to have children because they both liked their freedom, and Fran didn't want to be saddled to any responsibilities. But Dennis was very insistent.

Finally Fran said, "I know that I'm going to wind up caring for this dog, Dennis. This is simply too much responsibility now." Dennis said nothing. Fran could see the disappointment in his eyes, and the look he gave her tugged at her heartstrings, so she compromised. She agreed to take the dog home while they tried to find its owner.

Just as they were leaving the gym, a little boy came up to them and said they should name the dog "Lucky." Dennis agreed, and he and Fran brought Lucky home. They immediately called the humane society to see if anyone had inquired about a lost black puppy. They also posted flyers and put a lost-and-found notice in the paper. Despite all their attempts, no one claimed the little dog.

During this time Fran became accustomed to having Lucky in the house. She found herself actually looking forward to seeing him, and she started to thoroughly enjoy their daily walks and playtime sessions. She soon found that thoughts of Lucky occupied her mind and that the dog began to fulfill those dormant maternal instincts. In fact, the more she began caring for Lucky and receiving his love in return, the more she wanted to make him a permanent part of her life. Two months after bringing Lucky home as a temporary guest, Fran and Dennis made the decision to keep him.

Caring for Lucky helped Fran understand that all along she simply wanted an opportunity to love on a different level, and he became the recipient of that special love. Fran started to plan her days so that the time she spent with Dennis and Lucky was as fun-filled and loving as possible. Today, the three of them go for long walks and play ball together. Each evening, after Dennis and Lucky share some frozen yogurt, Lucky nuzzles with Fran and sleeps by her side. Lucky's love, affection, and companionship filled a void in Fran's life and freed her to use her heretofore untapped maternal instincts.

A New Feather to the Nest

Neal and Carolyn were devoted parents who always supported and nurtured their two children, Jay and Krista.

The children were close in age, and they had a strong bond and always strove to do things together. Their closeness filled their parents with relief because they knew the siblings would always look after one another.

After the oldest child went off to college, Neal and Carolyn began anticipating the fun they'd have as a couple again. They envisioned a quiet house without all the hustle and bustle of high school teenagers running in and out, vacations for just the two of them, and romantic evenings on the back porch. After the youngest left for college, Neal and Carolyn were ready for empty-nest life. What they had failed to anticipate, though, were their feelings of loneliness.

After spending 21 years raising and nurturing their children, they suddenly felt empty, and they questioned their past joyful view of life after child rearing. The quiet house, once filled with after-school study groups and weekend slumber parties, was now a silent reminder of the important role their children had played in their lives. As each day passed, they felt more and more disconnected from their lives and yearned for a way to make things "normal" again.

The two talked about their feelings and decided that they simply needed a little time to get used to the now quiet house. As time passed, though, the emptiness didn't go away. Instead, the silence became even more deafening than the music their children used to blare on the stereo. After a couple of years, Neal and Carolyn knew they had to do something.

Carolyn thought hard about a solution. Then she remembered that right after she and Neal married, they used to play with her father's German shepherd. They loved playing with Sammy and had a lot of fun visiting him. She remembered that they felt that on some level, the animal added to their lives. When Carolyn shared this idea with Neal, his immediate response was, "What would we do with a dog now?" But Neal and Carolyn discussed the topic openly and often after that, and they finally decided to go ahead. A dog might be just what they needed to fill the void in their life.

Within a few weeks, Neal and Carolyn found Millie—a beautiful two-year-old black-and-white Irish springer spaniel. The couple fell in love with her the moment they saw her and eagerly welcomed the dog into their home. Because both Neal and Carolyn worked full time outside the home, Carolyn as a schoolteacher and Neal as an administrator, Neal had been hesitant about bringing a dog into their lives. And neither Neal nor Carolyn had ever before had an indoor dog. "What if we can't give her the attention she needs?" Neal thought. "What if she becomes too much of a responsibility? What if her presence only makes us miss the children more?"

Neal and Carolyn soon discovered that his fears were unfounded. In fact, the love Millie so freely gives comforts both Neal and Carolyn in times of need and loneliness. Millie's presence fills them with a new love. Her tender kisses, happy bark, and wagging tail warm their hearts each day. And while they still miss their children deeply, Millie is helping them bridge the gap. They have learned that they can direct their attention to others for the love and companionship they desire. They scratch, rub, pet, and talk to Millie, comforted that someone still depends on them for nurturing.

Millie helped Neal and Carolyn so much and was such a joy in their lives that they decided another dog was a must. So less than three years after Millie's arrival, they added Annie, an eight-month-old brown-and-white English springer spaniel, to the family. They love having the two dogs, and they marvel at the dogs' unconditional love and support. Neal has noticed that Carolyn is more relaxed and less emotional and reactive, and both Neal and Carolyn believe that Annie's presence has helped them become a closer family by allowing them all to feel needed and loved. "Annie is keeping us all young," says Neal, "even Millie."

⟨⟩

The Mirror to Our Souls

VERY OFTEN our companion animals are a reflection of us. The love and friendship we receive so willingly from our furry, scaled, and feathered friends is what many of us wish we could show to others on a consistent basis. We live through the animals' affection vicariously, soaking up the wisdom they offer and attempting to put it to good use. We want to believe we can give of ourselves as unselfishly as they do, but the sad reality is that many of us simply don't. How can we love unconditionally in a society that places so much emphasis on our separating ourselves from each other? Unconditional love requires that we accept others and ourselves without judgment. It means that we offer others the freedom to be who they are in that moment and fully accept where they are in the unique process of their life. And it means that we allow ourselves the same freedom and acceptance. It's a lesson we need to learn if we want to live more meaningful and connected lives.

PET LESSON #1:

UNCONDITIONAL LOVE AND FRIENDSHIP

Exercises: How to Use This Pet Lesson in Your Everyday Life

1. Pick a person in your life that you are having difficulty loving unconditionally. Even if it's hard, think

about what strengths they have. How can you focus more on their positive attributes while minimizing the things that bother you? Like the animals did in some of the stories, try just being with that person without judging them.

2. One of the times you're the most natural is when you're with your companion animal. Remember the way you feel when you're in your pet's company, and picture yourself basking in their love and friendship. Like Tom when he was with Tara, let your heart soften and open up. Keep that feeling with you in your daily life to foster positive mental energy and promote self-assurance and self-love. Now bring to mind a situation going on in your life that is difficult to deal with: How would your pet see the situation?

3. When have you been accepted unconditionally? What was the situation? How did it feel? How can you extend this to others?

4. How does your companion animal make you feel friendly and caring? List the behaviors. How can you apply these to the way you judge yourself and to the way you deal with others?

5. Have you ever had a memorable experience with a companion animal? Try to remember the details. What do you feel was the lesson? Are you living your life now in a way that shows you've learned from this pet lesson?

CHAPTER TWO

Lessons of Loyalty and Trust

"The greatest pleasure of a dog is that you may make a fool of yourself with him and not only will he not scold you, but he will make a fool of himself, too."

—SAMUEL BUTLER

THINK BACK to some of the happiest moments in your life. For many people, images of weddings, birthdays, and holidays come to mind. The closeness of family and friends makes us feel happy and safe, and we often cherish those occasions that bring us together.

We humans instinctively seek the comfort of others to experience closeness. When we develop relationships that are based on trust or shared values, a sense of loyalty permeates the bond. This sense of loyalty occurs in nearly every societal structure, and it has the power to unite even strangers to pursue a common goal. When loyalty erodes, whether in the home or the workplace, loneliness and depression usually follow.

When married partners no longer feel loyal to each other, divorce is the usual course of action. From November 1998 through October 1999, 41 percent of marriages in the United States ended in divorce.[1] Glenn T. Stanton, author of the

21

book *Why Marriage Matters: Reasons to Believe in Marriage in Post-Modern Society*, found that people who have gone through a divorce are 20 percent more likely to experience depression, loneliness, and general mental illness.[2] Given the author's definition of loneliness as being the "absence of satisfying social relationships," as opposed to merely the close presence of other people, this finding is even more striking because it extends beyond only those who have experienced divorce—there are many people whose lives lack satisfying social relationships. Also, as one would expect, this erosion of marital loyalty has severe consequences on children—children of divorced couples are 50 percent more likely to develop health and psychological problems.[3]

Loss of loyalty in the workplace can be just as detrimental, affecting employee morale, productivity, and customer service. Through restructuring, downsizing, and overemphasis of the bottom line, company managers reduce employees' trust and loyalty. Additionally, as the gap in pay between executives and workers continues to widen, workers feel taken advantage of. At the same time, employers complain that employees don't display the same loyalty they once did and that their work ethics are at an all-time low. Through my consulting work with companies, I have often seen the negative impact that lost loyalty creates: Good employees leave disheartened, valuable customers go elsewhere, and profits go down. Everybody loses. But organizations that are loyal to their employees usually receive that same loyalty in return, and the workplace becomes a rewarding and enjoyable environment. And interestingly, employee loyalty breeds customer loyalty, so, in the end, everybody wins.

Loyalty and trust play a larger part in our personal and professional lives than most people realize. When we feel commitment and loyalty from friends, family, and coworkers, our self-esteem increases, and our relationships become more harmonious. We feel supported and experience less stress in our lives. Most people report that being in the presence of someone who is loyal is freeing. Sharing similar values—for example, the desire to learn, the need to grow, respect for others—can bring together diverse groups and build intense loyalties. Most people yearn for loyal connections in their lives, and being a part of a group of people who share similar outlooks on life can strengthen a person's sense of well-being and commitment to the particular cause or way of life. Whether you join the local country club, a Harley-Davidson riding group, or your company's softball team, you're extending yourself to reach out and form bonds in some way.

But humans aren't the only species that exhibit this sense of loyalty. Animals, too, are loyal to each other and to their human companions. In fact, as years pass and friends come and go, it is often our companion animals who remain by our sides and who live on in our memories long after their passing. One recent study conducted in Colorado nursing homes showed that animals had a positive impact on the social interactions of the residents.[4] The researchers go on to point out that 75 percent of the men and 67 percent of the women in this study stated that their dogs were their only friends.

Our companion animals can help us learn what being loyal really means. Their consistent loyalty is a model for the ongoing loyalty we all need in order to feel supported in life. They forgive us for any wrongdoings, and when that fuzzy, wagging tail or those big feline eyes greet us day in and day out, regardless of any of our past indiscretions, it makes us question the validity of the long-standing grudge we may hold against a friend or family member. What would happen if we let go of the anger we feel toward those who have hurt or betrayed us and instead stood true, held fast to our loyalty to them?

Through our companion animals, not only can we learn how to be loyal, but we can also learn the value of loyalty and its effect on humanity. And through our companion animals, we can discover ways to strengthen our commitments to each other, to other creatures, and to ourselves.

One doesn't need to observe or talk to people who live with animals very long to learn that the companion animal has a special role in their lives. Dr. Murray Bowen conducted a research study to try to determine the reason for the wide extent of pet ownership. Although the study found no single explanation, loyalty and companionship ranked very high. This was especially true with children, with the elderly, and with people who were vulnerable to loneliness following a major life change.[5] Whether it was death, divorce, or departure of children from home, the companion animal's steady presence served as a constant in an otherwise disrupted life.

Loyalty in the Face of Danger

Just as many humans strive to show their loyalty to each other by giving help when needed, so, too, do animals. Such was the case with Max, a small black-and-white pit bull who was unusually friendly and loved the three children—ages 7, 10, and 12—he lived with.

The family lived in the country, far from the nearest school and not on any bus route, so Melody would drive her children to and from school each day. Usually Max came along on these rides, but on this particular day Melody needed to go grocery shopping on her way home, so she left Max behind.

When Melody pulled up with the groceries, she turned the truck's ignition off and, glancing out the window as she was about to get out, saw that Max was ferociously growling and barking at her. Melody was shocked—Max had never displayed anything but loving behavior in the four years he had lived with them. She looked out the window again, hoping to find something or someone he was barking at, but she saw nothing. She thought, "Maybe Max will calm down once I get out of the truck."

As Melody reached for a bag of groceries from the backseat and started to open the door, Max became even more agitated. He bared his teeth at her and growled louder. Melody put the grocery bag back down and opened the door. Just as she was saying, "Oh, Max!" she spotted a coiled rattlesnake about to attack. Max lunged at the snake, instinctively protecting Melody.

The snake bit Max in the face. He yelped, and Melody screamed. She ran from the truck, grabbed a rake from the side of the house, and pushed the snake away. She picked up Max, put him in the truck, and drove him to the vet, who, fortunately, was only five minutes away. The vet treated the snakebite immediately. Max was sick for several weeks, but he recovered fully.

Both Melody and Max were shaken by the incident, and for weeks after, the entire family showered extra attention on Max. Melody still gets emotional when she thinks about the loyalty Max displayed in the face of a formidable foe and how he showed her how much he truly cares.

The Loyalty Connection

Animals do have feelings, and they do show emotion to other creatures, whether within their own species or to their human companions. In his book, *Kindred Spirits*, Dr. Allen Schoen, a veterinarian, brilliantly lays out the facts—animals have a clear capacity for love and loyalty.[6] Amazingly, there are those who still find this issue controversial. Skeptics tend to dismiss the human–animal relationship as forced or contrived. Some even argue that animals' stature in society has risen unjustly. Many of these doubters believe that the valuable attributes some of us strive to learn from animals are not so much attributes as random, meaningless behaviors.

Yet the fact is that every species exhibits signs of loyalty. What exactly is loyalty? When asked, many people define loyalty as being faithful and trustworthy. While that's correct as far as it goes, it's time we expand the definition to include "staying true to a person or belief despite contradictory conditions, supporting a friend even if you don't agree with something he or she is doing, remaining with a loved one in the face of adversity." In the animal world, being loyal means staying with the pack through times of feast or famine and remaining with a companion regardless of the circumstances.

In their book, *When Elephants Weep*, Jeffrey Moussaieff Masson and Susan McCarthy share a story about a game warden in Tanzania doing "elephant control work." Since his job was to keep the elephant population down, when the game warden saw three female elephants and a half-grown male in the tall grass, he thoughtlessly shot and killed the females and slightly wounded the half-grown male. Too late, the game warden saw two elephant calves hidden in the grass who had been with the females. He tried to move the calves along by shouting and waving his hands and hat, but they wouldn't budge. The two small elephants went to the wounded and dazed male. They pressed themselves against him in order to provide support, and then led him away from this dangerous and tragic situation back to safety.

When presented with scenarios such as these, most people can't help but believe that animals have an irrefutable sense of loyalty. Consider the story of Lady and Orson Wells, two adult shepherd mix dogs who shared an amazing bond of loyalty. Any one of us would be very lucky to experience such a bond even once.

Lady and Orson's Story

Liz and her mother, Lifa, were lifelong animal lovers who took in strays and helped them whenever they could. Whether an animal needed food, water, or medical attention, Liz and Lifa gave of themselves freely. So when two dogs showed up in their front yard—a yellow one and a skinny white one—it wasn't unusual that the women gave them assistance.

The first time the dogs arrived, Liz put some food and water out for them. Despite their obvious hunger, the dogs waited to eat until Liz closed the door. As soon as the coast was clear, the white dog (the female) came out of the bushes and ate first. The yellow dog (the male) ate what remained, then they left. This routine continued for several weeks. Each time, the yellow dog barked to make their presence known while the white dog hid in the bushes until food and water were put out. After a month of feeding the animals, Liz and Lifa decided to "walk" the two dogs home, hoping they would lead them back to their owners.

They followed the dogs several miles through the neighborhood and across busy roads. After about 20 minutes, the dogs entered a fenced yard with an open gate. Several children were playing in the yard. Lifa knocked on the door and was greeted by an older man with graying hair. She explained the situation with the dogs and how the dogs had led her to his house. Since she knew the dogs crossed three busy intersections to get to her house, she asked the man if he would keep the gate closed so the dogs couldn't escape and get hit by a car. The man refused and blamed the "white dog," as he referred to her, for their continually escaping. He seemed to grow impatient with Lifa and became abrupt with her. "Besides," he said, "they'll just jump the fence anyway." He concluded by telling Lifa to stop feeding the dogs if she didn't want them hanging around.

Lifa was concerned about the dogs' well-being and offered to spay and neuter the dogs so the man wouldn't eventually have puppies to worry about. The man replied that he didn't want the white dog and could care less if animal control picked her up, and he didn't want "the yellow one's 'thingies' to get cut off." Exasperated, Lifa left. The next day, the two dogs returned to her house.

This time, instead of feeding them, Liz and Lifa reluctantly took the dogs back to their original home, with the intention of making it a decent shelter for them with their original owner. The women filled the dogs' empty dishes with food, changed their fly-infested water, and made a makeshift shelter for them, since they had none. This pattern continued for months, with Lifa feeding them upon their routine arrival during the day and Liz taking them back home at night.

Their neighbors sometimes called animal control when they saw the two dogs roaming the neighborhood. Liz and Lifa explained to the animal control worker what was going on. He sympathized with the dogs' plight and knew that if he took them in they would be euthanized. So instead of taking them in, he, too, would follow them home in his car, keeping them safe through the busy intersections. But he told Liz and Lifa that they would have to find the two dogs a safe, permanent home. Liz and Lifa agreed to do so.

For the next few weeks, the women talked to everyone they knew about the dogs, but no one wanted them. They put up flyers in the neighborhood, offering the dogs to a loving home, and they even left word with all the local vets about the two dogs. Despite their efforts, they couldn't find anyone willing to take the two dogs. Liz and Lifa worried about the two dogs' future.

One day, only the yellow dog showed up. He came running up the front walkway barking and howling. Liz thought that perhaps he was especially hungry, so she put out some extra food. He refused to eat and danced nervously, looking off in the direction of his home. Lifa and Liz followed him. When they arrived at the house, the owner was gone for the day, and the white dog's back legs and neck were tightly tied with a coarse old rope, and she had no food, water, or shelter. Of course, Lifa's immediate reaction was to free the poor dog.

Normally quite active, both dogs sat patiently while she worked at the knots for 20 minutes. By the time she was done, her hands were bruised and bleeding but covered with dog kisses galore. The ordeal ended with the white dog howling, "Roo, roo, roo."

That day, Liz and Lifa decided to take the dogs. They waited on the man's front steps until he came home. When they asked for his permission to keep the dogs, he agreed. The women took the dogs home, wondering what their next step should be. They thought about keeping the dogs themselves but decided it would be impractical given the small size of their house. The dogs needed room to run, and their modest home could never accommodate two large dogs on a permanent basis.

The next day, Liz received a mailing from Best Friends Animal Sanctuary in Utah. After reading the literature and discovering that Best Friends is a place for abused animals to live out the rest of their lives in a loving environment, they called to see if they could bring the two dogs there. They explained the situation to the sanctuary worker, and the dogs were immediately accepted. The next week, Liz and Lifa drove the animals from California to Utah.

Once at Best Friends, the white dog was named Lady and the yellow dog was named Orson Wells. Liz and Lifa completed the necessary paperwork and, with tearful good-byes, left for home. The next week Lady and Orson were spayed and neutered. Orson recovered within a few days and was moved to a run with new friends, but something was wrong with Lady. She wasn't moving around well, and she didn't want to eat. The staff decided they needed to do further tests.

The next day, Lady couldn't get up at all. After reviewing her x rays and blood work, the doctors diagnosed her with fibrocartilaginous embolic myelopathy, paralysis of the hind legs that comes on suddenly with no apparent explanation. In Lady's case, the doctors surmised that it was caused by the trauma of having been tied up.

The doctors watched helplessly as Lady gave up her will to live. She ate and drank only enough to survive, and she never moved. Her only bright moments were visits from Orson, whose routine was eating breakfast, then running to see her at the clinic. He would stay by her side all day, intently watching what people were doing to Lady and kissing them if Lady gave him a look that told him she was not in pain.

One morning Lady couldn't even pick her head up, so the staff brought Orson over to see her. Orson immediately began showering Lady with kisses. Instantly her eyes lit up, and she gave her tail a short wag. The doctors were deeply touched by this display of emotion between the two animals. With a staff of eight standing around the two dogs, they vowed, with tears in their eyes, that if Lady got better, they would work it out so the two dogs would never be separated again.

Just then, Lady picked up her head. The spark in her eye was still there, and she gave a short, quick bark that seemed to say "Thank you." All of the workers experienced this show of emotion and had never seen such a look of gratitude from two dogs before. Shortly after, Lady began to heal. The doctors couldn't explain her sudden good health, but they didn't question it.

During Lady's recovery, the two dogs took up residence in a clinic recovery room with blankets and toys scattered throughout. They chose a small, pink stuffed animal as their favorite toy and would gingerly pass it back and forth and carry it around as if it were a baby. The two drank at the same time, but Orson, always the gentleman, would wait for Lady to eat her food before he would eat his. He was her bodyguard, always lying in front of her to ensure that no more harm would come to her. Each night before bed, the dogs could be found with their paws crossed over one another, always touching.

Everyone who met Lady and Orson quickly fell in love with them, and volunteers at the hospital would request to work with them for days at a time. Lady slowly improved with medicine, acupuncture, acupressure, and daily massage therapy. She put on weight and eventually was ready to go to a blanketed outdoor adoption run. Even there, burly Orson still insisted on lying outside their doghouse to guard her each night.

A few months later, the doctors decided that Lady needed to go to Colorado State University for special surgery to relieve pressure on her spinal cord and improve her walking ability. The trip was planned for the following week. Orson made the entire trip—from Utah to Colorado and back to Utah—and he stayed with Lady throughout her recovery.

Today, Lady has 100 percent use of one rear leg and about 70 percent use of the other. She thoroughly enjoys her daily walks and happily trots on-lead with her walker, with Orson off-lead and never more than a few feet away. If he ventures too far, Lady becomes worried and agitated, and Orson always comes back with a kiss for worrying her.

If you look into Lady's amber eyes, you see the love, respect, and loyalty she has for the lop-eared companion who saved her life. Many of the hospital staff believes that these two dogs were meant to be together forever and that fate sent them to Best Friends, where they happily reside, waiting for that very special home. Lady and Orson Wells are two gentle souls whose love and loyalty for each other affect all who meet them.

Animal researchers assert that relationships between humans and companion animals often mirror and extend family relationships. In a 1988 study conducted by Catherine T. Harris, Ph.D., of Wake Forest University, 502 veterinary clients were surveyed.[7] Harris found that clients were likely to comment that the companion animal was a "member of the family" or to use companionship imagery when describing the animal, such as "a trusted friend" or "a faithful companion."

A more recent study went a step further, actually analyzing dogs' loyalty to their human companions with M.D. Ainsworth's Strange Situations Test.[8] The study, conducted in Hungary, observed 51 owner and dog pairs. Each pair was tested with seven episodes that involved varying degrees of owner–dog interaction, owner–dog separation, and stranger–dog interaction. The findings are not surprising. When separated from their owner, the dogs spent more time standing by the door than when the owner was present. Furthermore, dogs sought more contact with their entering owner than with a stranger. The dogs also sought contact more quickly when their owner entered than when a stranger entered.

The results of this study demonstrate that adult dogs show patterns of attachment behavior toward the owner. A definite bond existed between the humans and the dogs, and the dogs sought the company of their caregivers over that of a stranger. Although there was a lot of variation in the dogs' attachment to humans, the researchers did not find that gender, age, living conditions, or breed had any effect on most of the behavioral variables.

Faithful Companions

PERHAPS ONE of the best examples of animal loyalty and human attachment can be found in the K9 police force, that is, police dogs. One study of 255 police officers found that the majority of officers enjoyed working with their canine partner and thought the dog was a favorable companion.[9] More than a third of the officers reported that the canine had saved the officer's life. Another third noted that a life-and-death situation had not yet arisen for them, although some stated that their canine partner had saved them from injury, and others felt that the canine might have positively influenced the behavior of some suspects.

It's interesting to note that the loyalty bond transcends the workplace. Although these dogs are adept at intimidating suspects while on duty, at home these dogs assume the role of companion. In fact, dog–officer relationships at home appear to be similar to those reported with companion dogs. They play together, the human officer converses with the canine officer and spends time grooming the animal, and, despite their large size, more than a third of the police dogs in the study slept in their officer partner's bedroom.

Many police officers who have a canine companion have so much trust in their dogs that they actually prefer their canine partner to a human partner. Cero was one such trusted dog.

Badge of Honor

A four-year-old Belgian Malinois who had been on the police force for a year and a half, Cero was strong and agile and a highly skilled law enforcement officer. His partner, officer Phil Monte, played a key role in choosing the dog and training him for police work. The two were inseparable at home and at work, and Officer Phil considered Cero the best partner a police officer could ever have.

In the early hours of a cold January morning, Officer Phil received a dispatch call informing him of an armed robbery in progress at a local business. Officer Phil and Cero were the closest unit to the location, so Phil responded that he and Cero were on the way. The dispatcher warned that the suspect was considered dangerous and that they were to use all means necessary to apprehend the perpetrator.

A 10-year veteran of the force, Phil was accustomed to dangerous work. He had been shot at and, several times, had come face-to-face with dangerous fugitives. Each time he had used extreme caution—he knew that this time would be no different. He also felt confident that Cero would protect him and would do his job if the need arose.

When Phil and Cero arrived, the suspect was fleeing the scene. He was running toward a chain-link fence that ran along the back edge of the building's property. Phil jumped out of his car, opened the back door for Cero to get out, pulled out his gun, and yelled for the suspect to stop. The suspect paused, and Phil thought he was going to comply, but then he saw that the suspect was drawing his weapon. Phil again yelled for the suspect to stop, then announced that he would let the dog loose. The perpetrator ignored the warning, pointed his weapon at Phil, and shot.

At that instant, Phil ducked and released Cero to apprehend the suspect. Sensing that his partner was in danger, Cero attacked the perpetrator. As Cero's teeth plunged into the suspect's leg, the man shot point-blank at the dog. Four bullets hit Cero, in the back and a rear leg. Despite his injuries, Cero remained loyal to his duties—even after being shot four times, he continued his attack and diverted the suspect's attention. This gave Phil time to return fire. The perpetrator was shot in the chest and subsequently taken into custody.

Phil called for backup and an ambulance. Cero was rushed to a local animal hospital, but they were unable to stabilize him, so they airlifted him to a university veterinary hospital 90 miles away. Cero recovered, remaining there for four weeks, but due to the severity of his injuries, it's doubtful that he will return to police work.

Cero now resides permanently in Phil's home. "Cero's loyalty and bravery saved my life that morning," says Phil. "I will continue to do all I can for him and remain as loyal to him as he was to me."

An Ageless Truth

THERE'S LITTLE DOUBT that because of their loyalty, companion animals have been and always will be important members of the family unit, whether that unit is two parents and three kids, an elderly grandmother who lives alone, a widower and his two children, or any other of the many variations that make up a family. According to some researchers, animals fulfill seven critical needs for people: They give us something to care for; they keep us busy; they are something to touch; they are something to watch; they make us feel safe; they provide a stimulus to exercise; and they provide companionship.[10] One study in particular noted that 96 percent of the respondents described their pet's role in the family as very important, clearly asserting that their companion animals contributed to the family's overall quality of life in a positive way. The researcher noted that the animals seemed to satisfy the basic human need for a loyal companion.[11]

Evidence of the loyalty and companionship people receive from their pets goes back thousands of years. The following example is more than a hundred years old. It is part of a court oratory presented in 1870 by a U.S. senator. It epitomizes the lesson of loyalty we can learn from our animal friends.

"The best friend a man has in the world may turn against him and become his enemy. His son or daughter that he has reared with loving care may prove ungrateful. Those who are nearest and dearest to us, those whom we trust with our happiness and our good name, may become traitors to their faith.

The money that a man has, he may lose. It flies away from him, perhaps when he needs it most. A man's reputation may be sacrificed in a moment of ill-considered action. The people who are prone to fall on their knees to do us honor when success is with us may be the first to throw the stone of malice when failure settles its clouds upon our heads.

"The one absolutely unselfish friend that man can have in this world, the one that never deserts him, the one that never proves ungrateful or treacherous, is his dog. A man's dog stands by him in prosperity, in health and sickness. He will sleep on the cold ground when the wintry winds blow and the snow drives fiercely, if only he may be near his master's side. He will kiss the hand that has no food to offer; he will lick the wounds and sores that come from encounters with the roughness of the world. He guards the sleep of his pauper master as if he were a prince. When all other friends desert, he remains. When riches take wings and reputation falls to pieces, he is as constant in his love as the sun in its journey through the heavens.

"If fortune drives the master forth, an outcast in the world, friendless and homeless, the faithful dog asks no higher privilege than that of accompanying him to guard against danger and to fight his enemies. And when the last scene of all comes and death takes the master in its embrace, and his body is laid away in the cold ground, no matter if all other friends pursue their way, there by the graveside will the noble dog be found, his head between his paws, his eyes sad, but open in watchfulness, faithful and true even in death."

This moving speech is attributed to Senator George Graham Vest, who delivered it during the 1870 court case *Burden v. Hornsby* in Warrensburg, Missouri. Senator Vest's oratory (this is only a portion of the speech; the latter half has been lost) was credited for winning the case for Charles Burden, whose favorite dog, Old Drum, had wandered onto the property of Burden's neighbor, Leonidas Hornsby. Hornsby made good his promise to shoot the first dog that wandered onto his property—that dog being Old Drum. He did this even though he had hunted with the dog and acknowledged the dog to be one of the best he'd ever hunted with.

Burden sued Hornsby for damages. Following several appeals, the case reached the Missouri State Supreme Court. Burden received an award of $50 in damages for the loss of his canine. The Warrensburg Chamber of Commerce and dog lovers around the county erected a statue of Old Drum on the lawn of the Johnson County Courthouse on September 23, 1958. It is said that this speech provided the origin of the phrase "A man's best friend is his dog." Of course, a woman's or child's best friend can also be a dog—or a cat, a horse, a ferret, a bird, a snake, and on and on.

The Feline Companionship Factor

WHILE THIS CHAPTER has given much attention to the loyalty of dogs, it's important to note that cats can be just as loyal and helpful as their canine counterparts. Granted, cats don't have the distinction of being "man's best friend," and have the reputation of sometimes being aloof, but they do become attached to their human companions and exhibit great loyalty as well. In some instances, cats can even learn their companion's schedule and keep their caregiver on track. That's exactly what Anne noticed in her feline companion, Spot.

Wake-Up Call

Anne became Spot's caregiver through an act of fate. Spot, a black cat with a white nose, white paws, and a white mark on his chest (hence the name), lived next door to Anne. He was a feral cat but had been "adopted" by Anne's neighbors, who fed him every day. Despite the neighbors' caring for him, Spot insisted on coming into Anne's yard to play and sleep.

At first Anne wasn't thrilled with the cat being in her yard, but she grew accustomed to him. She enjoyed watching him roll in the grass and chase field mice. She would often look out her back window and see him sleeping peacefully in a pile of leaves. Watching the cat always gave her a sense of serenity.

Spot's attachment to Anne's yard proved so deep that when the neighbors moved across town and took Spot with them, he refused to stay. He returned to his old neighborhood and took up residence in Anne's yard. Anne called her former neighbors, and they retrieved him, but again Spot returned to Anne's house. It was apparent to all concerned that Spot wanted to stay in his old neighborhood with Anne. She agreed and took over the duties of feeding this persistent cat.

At the time, Anne was head of a hospice in her community and had a very hectic schedule. She had always struggled with being a very sound sleeper. Frequently, she would set two alarm clocks, knowing that she would often shut off one alarm in her sleep and never remember doing it. And because she lived alone, there was no one else to wake her.

As Spot grew more at ease with Anne, he would approach her and let her pet him. Once they were both comfortable with that arrangement, Anne allowed Spot to come in the house. At first he slept in a cat bed in the living room, but after a few months he began to venture into Anne's bedroom. Eventually, he was sleeping in Anne's bed with her, and he became accustomed to her habits. Whenever the first alarm clock would go off, he'd begin nuzzling her. When the second alarm clock would go off a few minutes later, he would start licking her hand and patting at her chest. He was always very gentle and loving.

One morning, after getting very little sleep the night before, Anne rolled over in her sleep and turned off the screeching alarm clock. As usual, Spot came over and started to nuzzle. Unfortunately, Anne's backup alarm clock was not set properly and never went off. To make matters worse, this was a very important day for Anne. She had a full schedule of meetings, and family members of one of the patients were flying in to meet with her first thing in the morning.

Spot, who realized that Anne's second alarm should have gone off, began licking Anne's hand. When that didn't get her attention, he began patting at her chest. Still there was no response from Anne, so Spot got aggressive. He jumped on Anne's chest and began hitting her gently in the face with his paws. When Anne slowly opened her eyes, Spot jumped from Anne's chest over to the alarm clock and knocked it off the bureau. At first Anne was furious and yelled, "Spot! Stop it! What's wrong with you?" But after regaining her composure, she saw what time it was and realized that without Spot's waking her, she would have slept through her important meeting. Spot proved his loyalty to Anne that day, and she now considers him more dependable than any alarm clock she has ever owned.

The Catalyst for Self-Reflection

NO ONE CAN DENY that life is more enjoyable when we have a trusted companion by our side. We instinctively want someone available for support and understanding, someone who is dependable, trustworthy, and faithful. For many of us, a companion animal fills this role. The loyalty of animals and their ability to make us feel that we are needed and loved are perhaps the greatest gifts they can give.

By observing our companion animals, we can model the loyalty our animal friends show to each other and to their human companions. We have but to follow their example and we'll be better able to connect with our friends and family, thereby forging tighter bonds with our loved ones. Loyalty allows us to experience trust and support at home and at work. It helps us to weather unforeseen storms and encourages us to take a higher road in our daily lives and our interactions with others.

Being loyal means that we reach out to others, offering support in meeting life's challenges without expecting anything in return. It's a quality that many people have lost, having become too wrapped up in society's "succeed at all costs" mind-set. In the end, however, loyalty is the basis for any meaningful bond. In order to be loyal to others, however, we need to start by learning to trust ourselves and by following through on the commitments that we make to ourselves. An example of this is remaining loyal to what we see as our values. If honesty is important to us, then acting in alignment with that value increases self-trust and enhances our ability to be faithful to ourselves and to others. When we connect with ourselves and others in this very instinctive and personal way, we benefit from a "strength in numbers" mentality and a unity that can help us reach a new global level of human consciousness.

PET LESSON #2:
LOYALTY AND TRUST

Exercises: How to Use This Pet Lesson in Your Everyday Life

1. What makes you feel loyal and trusting? Think about an occasion when you either gave or received loyalty and trust. What happened? How are you applying these insights to your life on a daily basis?

2. Think about the loyalty between Lady and Orson. How can you apply this to the friendships in your life? What holds you back, if anything?

3. Max was brave to get bitten by the snake so that Melody wouldn't be injured. Are you willing to take a hit for others in your life? Why or why not?

4. How has your companion animal exhibited loyalty toward you? How can you model those behaviors with people in your personal and professional lives?

5. Have you ever experienced disloyalty or betrayal at work? Describe the situation and the result. How did this affect the way you trust yourself? The way you trust others?

6. Give an example of a loyal act that would increase your trusting others even more? What are some ways you can act on this insight?

7. Make a list of affirmations that reflect the way you'd like to see loyalty and trust playing a role in your life. Be as specific as possible; for example, "I am loyal to my friends and coworkers." Narrow your statements down to the few that seem most appropriate for you and write them repeatedly on a piece of paper.

CHAPTER THREE

Lessons of the Circle of Life

"It's a leap of faith, a band of hope, until we find our place on a path unwinding in the circle of life."

—ELTON JOHN

LIFE IS truly a miracle, and as such it's difficult, if not impossible, to understand. How did we get here? What are we here to do? What are our gifts and talents? How do we want to spend the time we have here? Why do we grow old? What happens when we die? These are all questions that have been challenging people for centuries. While none of us will ever know with absolute certainty the answers we seek, we can learn to adjust to and accept life's various and inevitable cycles.

These topics can be even more difficult for children to comprehend. As parents, we often feel that birth and aging and death are too overwhelming for children to understand, so we try to protect them by keeping these topics (or at least aspects of them) under wraps. But I believe that children benefit from learning about these things; that a basic understanding of the circle of life can contribute to children's mental

43

well-being and their eventual successful growth into adulthood. This understanding can begin with the companion animal in their life—that's why the pet lesson in this chapter is one our children should not miss.

An animal's life span is usually significantly shorter than a human's, so we can observe the entire circle of life, from birth to death, in a relatively short period of time. In the process, we can learn not only about key developmental traits, such as compassion, self-respect, responsibility, and trust, but also about the various phases of life. It is often through a companion animal that children first experience nurturing another creature and forging a lifetime bond that will inevitably end. By observing and interacting with companion animals, children receive a sort of dress rehearsal for life events that all of us go through.

In a different way, adults can also learn about life cycles through their companion animal—a pet can help adults get through a divorce, adjust to a return to school or any new lifestyle, or grieve the death of a loved one.

Companion Animals and Child Development

THROUGHOUT THE YEARS, some research has been done on the role that companion animals play in child development. As children develop and grow, animals serve as a support to the various developmental stages that children go through, such as building trust and self-esteem, feeling competent, reaching autonomy, and becoming more sensitive to the feelings of others.[1] Researchers have found that a child's interaction with animals changes in accordance to the child's age. For example, toddlers (two- to three-year-olds) more frequently engage in poking, prodding, and grabbing animals, while three- to four-year-olds are more likely to pet their animals than do anything else with them. Older children (five-to six-year-olds) generally hug, pet, stroke, and massage their animals. What's interesting to note is that the progression in how the children behave with animals often mirrors the development of the interactions they have with familiar humans, including parents, siblings, and peers.[2]

The reactions children have toward animals became evident to me when I heard the story of a brother and sister—Michael, age seven, and Hannah, age three. Being at different levels of social development, they behaved pretty differently with the little animals that came to live with them, but they both learned an incredible lesson about the will to live.

A Second Chance at Life

All his life, Michael wanted a pet. He didn't care whether it was a dog, a cat, a hamster, or a rabbit; he simply wanted an animal he could care for and call his own. From the time he learned to talk, he would beg his parents to allow him to bring an animal home. "I promise to feed it and take care of it," he'd say. Each time, his parents told him that they'd think about it.

For Michael's seventh birthday, his parents decided to fulfill his one and only wish. They were going to get him a pet. Because they wanted him to have a strong attachment to the animal, they didn't want to surprise him with just any old animal—they wanted him to pick out the pet he would love and care for.

When Michael and his parents went to the local pet store, they were a bit overwhelmed. As far as the eye could see there were puppies, kittens, ferrets, bunnies, and a host of other animals. The shopkeeper showed them around and cited the benefits of each animal choice. Elizabeth, Michael's mom, thought they'd be bringing home a puppy or kitten that day, but Michael surprised them all. He walked over to the rodent section of the pet store and screamed out, "I found it! I found it!" By the time his parents and the shopkeeper met him, Michael had already fallen in love with three female gerbils.

Elizabeth was both relieved and apprehensive. She was pleased that she wouldn't have to train a new puppy or kitten, especially since she already had her hands full with a seven-year-old and a three-year-old, but the idea of three gerbils running loose in her house didn't sit well. But she had promised Michael a pet of his choice, so despite her apprehension, they took the gerbils home.

Once home, Michael could hardly contain his happiness. He sat with his new gerbils for hours, petting them, nuzzling them, and talking to them as if they were humans. He showed the gerbils to Hannah and even let her hold them. He explained how gentle she had to be with them while she squealed with delight as the gerbil's furry body tickled her hand.

Michael played with his gerbils day and night. He talked with them in the morning before school, he watched them run in their cage after school, and when his mom wasn't looking, he'd even let the gerbils run loose in his bedroom. He was always gentle with the little animals and did his best to protect them from harm.

One day when Michael was at school, Hannah (who wasn't supposed to play with the gerbils unattended) and her friend, a little boy about her age, took the gerbils out of their protective home and brought them to the bathroom to play with them. Elizabeth was in the kitchen washing dishes when she heard an unmistakable "Uh-Oh" echoing from the bathroom. She ran to the bathroom to see what was going on. When she arrived, she saw Hannah and her little friend peering into the toilet. "What happened, Hannah?" she asked.

Hannah held her head down and pointed at the toilet. "They go down," was all she said. After some detective work, Elizabeth realized that, in the process of playing and not being as careful with the gerbils as her older brother, Hannah and her friend had flushed the gerbils down the toilet.

Elizabeth was livid. She immediately began plunging the toilet with the hopes the pressure would bring the gerbils up. It didn't work. Elizabeth gave up, not knowing what to do or what she was going to say to Michael. She was appalled that her daughter could do such a thing, and she explained to Hannah the seriousness of her actions.

When Michael came home that day after school, Elizabeth sat him down and explained, as best as she could, what had happened. "NO, NO, NO!" Michael yelled. He burst into tears and ran to his room. Inconsolable, he moped in his room for the rest of the day. Elizabeth offered to buy him more gerbils, but he declined her offer. He was mourning the loss of his close friends.

The next day, Michael was in the bathroom getting ready to take a shower. He was still depressed and didn't want to talk to Hannah at all. Just as he was about to turn on the shower water, he looked down and saw a tail coming up through the shower drain. He screamed as loud as he could, "Mom! One of the gerbils is back!"

Elizabeth, hearing her son's cry, was reluctant to go into the bathroom. She was sure he was just being wishful, sure there was no way a gerbil could survive in the pipes. She was wrong. There, in the drain, unmistakably, was the tail of a gerbil. Elizabeth and Michael looked at each other, excited, hardly daring to hope.

As Elizabeth dismantled the drain, one of the gerbils poked her face through the opening. Although she was dirty and sickly looking, her eyes had a certain spark. As soon as Michael saw her, he cried out, "It's Bright Eyes!" Michael grabbed her and took her to her cage to rest.

Michael stayed home from school that day and cared for Bright Eyes. He fed her water with a dropper and hand-fed her pieces of gerbil food. Slowly, Bright Eyes was regaining her strength. Within a few weeks, she was healthy enough for some company, so the family bought a male gerbil, which they named Bushy Tail. The two gerbils got along well—so well, in fact, that a litter was soon on the way.

Michael and Hannah were excited about the impending baby gerbils. Each day, they'd check on Bright Eyes to see how she was doing. When the day arrived that she went into labor, Elizabeth let them watch as she explained what was happening. Michael and his mother assert that after the birthing process, Bright Eyes looked up at them with love and thankfulness. It was as if she was saying, "Thank you for saving my life, giving me a second chance to live." They both sensed that her life was now complete.

The male and female gerbils were soon separated to keep them from multiplying further, and Michael raised them in two sets of cages, giving some of them to responsible friends. Michael's mom wholeheartedly believes that the lessons Bright Eyes taught the children about death, hope, and birth were invaluable to their maturation process.

The Child's Desire to Nurture

COMPANION ANIMALS positively impact the emotional development of children.[3] The constant presence and friendship of animals can assist children as they move through various stages in their growth. Levinson states companion animals may even minimize or inhibit mental difficulties or illness in children.[4]

Companion animals are seen as nurturing to children. Robin and ten Bensel discuss that pets display the characteristics of an "ideal mother" by being unconditional, loyal, and attentive.[5] In turn, children show nurturing behavior to their companion animals and can simultaneously view them as their children.[6] In a study about the human-animal companion bond in military communities, the majority of families surveyed believe that children should have companion animals while growing up.[7] The researchers concluded that most people believe that companion animals prepare children for later life experiences that relate to giving and receiving love, parenting, birth, and death. By successfully caring for a companion animal, children learn a sense of importance and feel needed.[8]

Perhaps one of the most profound impacts animals have on children is their ability to elicit feelings of nurturance. Studies in New York revealed that animals can stir parental behaviors in children as young as three years old. In these instances, the animal takes on the role of infant, and the child mimics the role of the parent. By doing this, children are essentially preparing for the loss of their childhood and learning basic nurturing skills necessary for later life.[9] Furthermore, the more children nurture, the stronger is their sense of trust. Evidence suggests that basic trust—a vital trait that children need while growing up in order to interact successfully with friends and family— stems from children's secure attachments to others, attachments that reassure children of their safety and provide them with a secure base. And when children nurture a companion animal, they form a secure attachment, which, in turn, contributes to their sense of basic trust.[10]

My Trusted Confidant

Like many of the people highlighted in this book, I, too, have a special story about my first animal companion. When I was a young girl, my life revolved around my cat Cookie. He was a large Maine coon who dominated the neighborhood. Birds and other cats fled as Cookie roamed his territory. The neighborhood children weren't overly fond of Cookie either, as he would often hiss at them and run when they tried to pick him up. But I had a special way with him. I could pick him up, play with him, hug him, and place wet kisses on his nose. Cookie knew that he belonged to me and I to him. The bond we had was unbreakable.

I remember many rainy afternoons when I would dress Cookie in my doll's pink clothes and giggle as he waited patiently to be released. Deep down I knew Cookie didn't enjoy these antics, but he was patient enough to let me play and learn. My older brother and sister couldn't believe that Cookie submitted to being pushed in a baby carriage as I regularly attended to my "baby."

I fondly recall the warm summer days in New England when I played for hours with my patient cat, who seemed to sense that I needed to learn something from his presence. Rainy days were my favorite because Cookie would stay indoors with me the entire time. We'd nuzzle on the couch and watch the raindrops hit the window, or we'd lie on the floor together, and his tender paws would swat at my face. He was my living baby doll, and I loved him more than anything. I sang my favorite songs of love to him—all the lullabies that my grandmother and my mother had taught me.

I trusted Cookie with all my secrets and made him promise not to tell anyone else, not even the family dog. When I talked to Cookie, I practiced what to say to my future children and to my future husband. Cookie allowed me to experiment and discover what to say and do, as I so wanted to learn how to be "grown up."

From Birth to Death

COMPANION ANIMALS can be valuable in educating children about life events. For example, animals can teach important lessons about birth and death. In many instances, the birth of a litter or the death of a family companion animal is a child's first experience with such occurrences. In fact, one of the most important aspects of an animal's influence on child development is that through an animal, a child can learn about the reality of birth and death and about the emotions associated with living and dying.[11]

A New Understanding of Birth

For most families, the birth of animals is an exciting event that gives parents an opportunity to explain how life begins and that can form a part of early sex education. David remembers the day he was sitting in front of the family fish tank and learned about birth and reproduction. He was six years old. While he was watching the velvet swordtails swim back and forth, one fish in particular caught his attention. She was hovering above a "grassy" patch in the tank and wiggling from front to back. When David put his face up to the tank, he noticed tiny baby fish darting around in the grassy area. The longer the female fish hovered there, the more baby fish that appeared.

Having just recently visited his aunt in the hospital, where she had given birth to his cousin, David had a vague idea of birth and babies. He got really excited and called for his mom. After she assessed the situation, she took the mother fish from the tank, putting her in a separate bowl. David asked why she was doing this, and his mother explained that if she kept the mother fish with the babies, the mother fish would eat them. Confused, David looked at his mom and asked, "Is that why they kept all those babies in a glass room at the hospital? So that the mommies don't eat them?" At that point, David's mom sat him down and gave him his first explanation, albeit condensed, of birth and reproduction. The birth of the baby fish was the catalyst for his being ready to learn about the miracle of life.

At the other end of the spectrum is death. This is a painful experience for children who are emotionally attached to the animal, but dealing with a pet's death is a necessary part of learning about the circle of life through our animals. Through the animal's death and the child's grieving process, children learn that death is a natural part of life and that the grief that follows is not permanent. When parents contribute to the learning experience by offering comfort and letting the child know that the grieving emotions of anger, denial, and guilt are normal, the child will be better prepared for future losses.

Unfortunately, as a society, we tend to discount a child's grief over the loss of an animal. While children of different ages react to death differently, their feelings are still very real. Robin and ten Bensel point out that how a child reacts to a companion animal's death depends not only on age and emotional development but also on the length of time the child knew the animal, the quality of the relationship, the circumstances of the animal's death, and the quality of emotional support available to the child.[12]

Universally, children under five years old understand that losing a companion animal is a significant family event, yet they don't realize that death is permanent. As a result, they might not cry about the loss initially—their symptoms of grief may come and go with varying degrees of intensity—but they may ask many questions about death.[13] School-aged children often express profound grief; however, they generally miss having a playmate more than being around a living creature that satisfies emotional needs.[14] By the time children reach adolescence, they realize that death is permanent and inevitable, and because adolescents are able to connect with an animal at a deeper emotional level, an animal's death generally hits this age group the hardest. Sometimes they hide their feelings, sometimes they act out their grief in the form of anger.[15]

Regardless of their age, children dealing with the loss of a pet need to be treated with respect. Adults should strive to be open and honest about the death and help the child work out feelings of grief. Parents should consider some sort of funeral or memorial service to lend an act of closure to the event. Even though our society has no set ritual for a companion animal's death, a small service helps children and adults heal. It also signifies to the family how important and how much a part of the family the animal was to them.

The Last Dance

When Paula's dog, Heidi, died, it affected her in a way no one could ever have imagined. Heidi, a German short-haired pointer, was Paula's first dog. She had become a part of the family when Paula was five years old. That same year, Paula began taking dance lessons. After every lesson, she'd run home to show Heidi what she had learned. She'd then put Heidi up on her hind legs so the two could dance together throughout the house.

Paula's fondest childhood memories are of her dog and her dance lessons. As Paula would dance around the house with Heidi, she'd recite the instructions from her dance teacher: "Step, one, two . . . and back, three, four." She was amazed at how Heidi seemed to know how to keep in step with the music. The two—Heidi and dance—were inextricably linked, and they were Paula's stability throughout grammar school, junior high, and high school.

By Paula's senior year of high school, Heidi had aged. She was far from the youthful puppy who used to dance with Paula. Heidi could no longer keep in step with the music. Her stiff joints made even walking increasingly difficult, and all she wanted to do was sleep.

Paula recalls the last time she saw Heidi—she was curled up like a swan in her parents' bedroom. She was wrapped in a pink blanket and did not move. Although Paula did not want to say good-bye to her best friend and dance partner, she knew that day would be Heidi's last dance. Heidi died later that evening.

Paula cried as her parents carried Heidi away. And when Heidi left, Paula's desire to dance left with her. With college just around the corner, she knew she had to devote more time to her studies and less time to dance. But even more profound, she had lost her favorite dance partner. No matter what music she played, Paula could not will her spirit to move to the beat. Without Heidi, dancing was no longer the same.

The days following Heidi's death were the most painful for Paula. She felt the need to be quiet, and she sat in her bedroom. She thought about where Heidi had gone after she died and, more important, about where she, herself, would go. She wondered about the purpose of life, about the purpose of love, and if a broken heart could ever truly mend. Heidi's death prompted her to begin questioning her own mortality, and for the first time, the notion of death actually scared her. She missed the feeling of protection she had when Heidi was around and the dancing that was so much a part of their relationship.

Paula never found the answers to the questions she pondered that day, but as time passed, she began to accept Heidi's death. She found out she could look back and learn from the experience. In many ways, Heidi's death prepared Paula for losses she would experience as life went on, including the deaths of her aunt, her mother-in-law, and her grandmother. By learning how to let go of Heidi, Paula was more able to let go of others.

"At five years old I had Heidi and joy," says Paula. "At 17 I lost her, and a piece of myself went with her, too. But once I was able to accept her death, her spirit permeated my soul. When that happened, I was able to dance again. Today I dance and I feel Heidi by my side. Both will always be a part of me, because with Heidi's death, I learned that we can heal any loss if given the time."

Companion Animals and Their Social Influence on Children

BEING ABLE to develop friendships and connect with others is important in life, and having a companion animal by our side can help. Think about it: An animal can increase social contact with strangers. Don't you find that people are more likely to talk to you when you're walking a dog than when you're walking alone? If you are visiting a home where cats are present, doesn't it make you more at ease or prone to strike up a conversation faster? Research shows that when unfamiliar people are in the presence of animals, they appear less threatening.[16] And as animals increase an adult's visibility, so, too, do they increase a child's visibility.

Research has been conducted around a companion animal's ability to help children form social bonds. One predominant theory is that companion animals enhance the attractiveness of the child as a friend or playmate.[17]

However, G. F. Melson points out that simply keeping a companion animal does not help children form bonds; rather, it's the attachment to the companion animal that is important. His research has shown that the depth of children's involvement with a companion animal is related to their involvement in non-school social activities. Children who have formed bonds with animals are more likely to participate in activities with others where human bonds are likely to develop.[18]

Breaking the Silence

Sometimes a companion animal helps children form bonds because the animal is a channel of communication for them. Such was the case with Sean. At age two, Sean (now nine years old) was diagnosed with high-functioning autism. People with Sean's form of autism usually learn to function fairly well in society, but, especially for children, there are severe social and linguistic barriers that must be overcome. Sean's social, language, and developmental skills were much less advanced than other children his age.

In an effort to help him develop the language and social skills he needed, Sean's mother, Rebecca, started introducing small animals into their home. This was a big step for Sean, as any change in his environment could trigger him to act out aggressively. Fish and frogs were first. Much to Rebecca's relief, Sean interacted well with the animals and strove to learn about them. The animals prompted Sean to speak, and he developed the ability to "share" the animals with the rest of the family.

When Sean reached eight years old, he began to progress in leaps and bounds. All of his stereotypical autistic movements, such as rocking and finger flicking, disappeared, and he made remarkable progress in his language skills. He was even able to carry on a simple conversation with family members. His thoughts and daily routines, however, remained somewhat rigid and obsessive.

One day, Rebecca decided to throw caution to the wind and bring home two young ferrets. She had ferrets while she was growing up and knew they had a good nature and positive behavioral attributes. When she brought the ferrets home, Sean was curious about them. He seemed disturbed, but he didn't get upset or hurt the animals. Under his mother's constant supervision, Sean became fascinated by and very protective of the ferrets. Slowly, he grew accustomed to the sights, sounds, and smells the animals brought into his home. He would watch the ferrets for hours, never once acting out toward them or hurting them. Having the ferrets around made it easier for Sean to connect with others, as he would use the ferrets as a catalyst for conversation. Sean's progress was so astounding that just a few months later his parents decided to give Sean a ferret of his own.

Wanting Sean to feel that the new animal was truly his, they allowed him to pick out the ferret of his choice. When they went to the pet store, Sean bonded immediately with a small black-and-white ferret. Sean named him Rocky, and the two were soon inseparable.

Rebecca has been amazed at how intimately Sean interacts with Rocky. He holds Rocky close to his face and talks to him about his deepest thoughts and feelings. As a result, Sean's language, development, and social skills have seen dramatic improvement. Sean has also learned about the nourishment, care, and maintenance Rocky requires and performs these chores responsibly every day. Sean has even joined a Little League baseball team, and Rebecca makes sure that Rocky attends every game.

Mary R. Shefferman, editor and cofounder of *Modern Ferret Magazine,* is not surprised by Sean's progress. As she explained, "Ferrets are small, quiet, good-natured, and intelligent pets. These are the qualities that make Rocky a particularly good companion for Sean. In fact, many people are drawn to ferrets because of these qualities."

Sean's prognosis is positive. As time goes on, he learns more and more about ferrets and takes on more responsibility. Sean spends hours every day talking to Rocky about everything from school and friends and family to his deepest fears and wishes. Rocky certainly helped bring out the positive qualities Sean has to offer the world.

Direct Influences of Companion Animals on Child Development

SOCIAL-EMOTIONAL DEVELOPMENT, which includes the ability to develop positive self-esteem, empathy toward others, responsibility, patience, and anger management, is another important aspect of children's maturation. Noted child psychologist Boris Levinson once remarked that raising companion animals can enhance children's empathy, self-esteem, self-control, and autonomy, and other researchers have reported a positive relationship between having a companion animal and children's degree of social sensitivity and interpersonal trust.[19]

How exactly can a companion animal foster feelings of self-esteem and autonomy? Consider this scenario. When there are companion animals in the house, the responsibilities for taking care of the animal are generally divided among the family members. For younger children, tasks can be as simple as giving an animal water, while older children may have responsibilities such as feeding, walking, or grooming the animal. Children of all ages learn how to care for and nurture a living creature that is totally dependent on the people in its life, then when they are praised for successfully completing age-appropriate tasks, self-esteem and a sense of belonging develop.

Also through this interaction with a dependent animal, children learn to understand the feelings and needs of animals and humans. They learn that not feeding or walking an animal has consequences—not only for themselves but also for the animal. And as they develop empathy for their animal's needs and feelings, they learn to have empathy for people as well.

Gentle Rehabilitation

Perhaps some of the greatest examples of the positive effects that companion animals have on a child's social-emotional development comes from programs that utilize animals in the juvenile rehabilitation process. One such organization, Associated Marine Institute (AMI), headquartered in Tampa, Florida, operates an alternative school for juvenile offenders in Melbourne, Florida, called the Space Coast Marine Institute. The school takes in troubled youths ages 14 to 18. All the youths have been convicted of one or more crimes and attend Space Coast Marine Institute in lieu of incarceration.

Two years ago, the institute added a canine companion program to their juvenile rehabilitation process. In the canine companion program, juveniles have the opportunity to care for and train service dogs. Wendell Watson, the program administrator, requires all juvenile residents interested in the program to go through a thorough application process that includes writing essays and being in compliance with all treatment plans in their rehabilitation process. Once accepted into the canine companion program, the youths receive an eight-week-old puppy to care for. They feed the puppies, walk them, groom them, and play with them, and they are responsible for taking the puppies to their veterinary appointments and training classes. The youths also take full responsibility for the puppies' actions—if a puppy causes any destruction or messes on school grounds, the juvenile caretaker is responsible for cleanup or repair. After the puppies reach four months old, they begin spending the night with the juveniles in the dormitory, and the youths take the puppies to class with them and to any other functions. At that point, the puppies are with the kids around the clock.

Wendell recalls the story of two boys, Brian and Terry. Both boys had been convicted of assault, and both had severe anger issues. They would fly off the handle at the smallest provocation. They had very little self-respect, and neither had any self-control or sense of responsibility. But Brian and Terry were accepted into the canine program, and once they began interacting with the puppies, a transformation occurred.

The more the boys interacted with the puppies, the more patience they developed and the more responsibility they were willing to take on. They quickly realized that the puppies were not well behaved 100 percent of the time, and that they had to adjust their behavior to match their assigned puppy's temperament and personality. As they developed a sense of empathy toward the puppies, the boys' anger slowly diminished. They let themselves be entertained by the puppies' antics. They began smiling and laughing more. And the more their individual puppy pro-gressed in the program—the more it learned—the higher the boys' sense of personal pride and accomplishment.

Both Brian and Terry graduated from the Space Coast Marine Institute. The lessons they learned while caring for the puppies—self-respect, empathy, responsibility, pa-tience, love, and understanding—have stayed with them, and today they are productive and law-abiding citizens.

The Space Coast Marine Institute's puppy program is growing, and Brian and Terry are now involved in training other juveniles about what they learned. In the two years since the institute implemented the canine program, they've experienced great success. To date, all the juveniles who have graduated from the program have successfully reentered society and have had no further run-ins with the law. Apparently, the puppies have a tremendous impact on the troubled youths and are a vital component to their emotional rehabilitation.

Adult Perceptions on the Circle of Life

IT'S IMPORTANT to note that children aren't the only ones who benefit from pet lessons about the circle of life. Adults go through many life changes, and our companion animals often help make the transition easier and stimulate our gain-ing insights from the experiences.

Letting Go of Yesterday

It's widely accepted that most adults understand concepts such as birth and death and that they have, to the extent possible, adjusted to their responsibilities and social-emotional developments. But there will still be times when they need a wake-up call to set them on the path they must follow in life.

John received such a call when two major life events occurred simultaneously. The wheels were set in motion when John, whose wife was often unavailable due to a chronic illness, gave his nine-year-old daughter, Dawn, a collie-terrier mix dog. The dog's coat reminded Dawn of the color of honey, so that's what she named her: Honey. Although Honey was to be Dawn's dog and responsibility, Honey formed the strongest bond with John.

Since Dawn was an only child, Honey was affectionately referred to as her "sister." The two girls were inseparable. When Dawn rode her bicycle after school, Honey would run alongside, barking and panting. Another of Honey's favorite games was keep-away—holding a squeaky toy in her mouth, Honey would run from Dawn, who would chase her all around the house and the backyard.

Over the years, John nurtured both Dawn and Honey, always keeping a watchful eye on his "daughters." But time passed, and Dawn began to grow up. John had a difficult time letting go, from the first small steps, like allowing her to walk past a certain point in the neighborhood, to larger issues, like dating and curfews. Despite John's desire to keep his daughter his "baby" forever, she did eventually meet a man whom she wanted to marry.

After Dawn got married, John felt empty. And as was his style, he refused to let his daughter grow up. He routinely offered to help pay some of her bills or do some repair work around her house, and he invited her over to dinner almost every night. Dawn's only solace—and only respite—was that he still had Honey to keep him company.

A month after Dawn's wedding, just as the phone calls were easing down to every other day and John was slowly beginning to let go, tragedy happened: Honey experienced complete liver failure and died. John was devastated, as now both his "girls" were gone from his home. Saying good-bye to Honey was the only time Dawn ever saw her father cry.

John was in a state of depression after Honey's burial. He moped around the house and didn't have any enthusiasm for life anymore. He became even more dependent on his daughter, calling her multiple times every day just to talk. But then an interesting thing happened. One day, a few weeks after Honey's death, John woke up with a vigor to begin investigating taking an entirely new path in life. When he told Dawn about his plans, she encouraged him to go for it. Soon, John began traveling—something he had done very little of—to places like the Virgin Islands, Las Vegas, and Hawaii. He started taking dance lessons and was soon able to rumba and cha-cha with ease. He sold his large, high-maintenance house and purchased a small condo on the beach. He also started investigating business opportunities, and within a few months, he quit his secure, longtime managerial job and opened his own retail establishment.

Dawn is convinced that Honey's death helped her father realize that the nurturing phase of his life was over and that he now needed to focus on himself and his dreams and ambitions. Since before Dawn's marriage, he had been so wrapped up in his "daughters" and in trying to hang on to the status quo, that he was unable to see the possibilities that awaited him. While he will always dearly miss the family's beloved dog, losing Honey, then letting go and moving on, transformed him into a whole new person.

Transitions and a Companion Animal

HAVING A companion animal by our side can make adult life transitions more bearable. A great number of people are apprehensive of change, and a companion animal's constant presence helps keep us rooted in the present while we embark on future adventures. The animal can provide a sense of comfort and stability.

A Shoulder to Lean On

Randy went through multiple life transitions in a matter of a few years. And throughout them all, she had her faithful friend Katie, a red Irish setter, at her side.

Randy and her husband, John, adopted Katie as a way of breathing life into their declining relationship. The romance they had once felt toward each other was dwindling, and they both believed that having something to love and nurture would rekindle those emotions. Unfortunately, they were mistaken. Although Katie was an instant joy in Randy's life, John wasn't thrilled with the animal. The couple continued to fight frequently—about the dog, about money, and about their relationship in general. Their arguing was not only hard on them but also hard on Katie. During the couple's fights, Katie would often sit by the door, shaking.

When the marriage did end, Randy decided that she needed to reinvent herself. Her first course of action was to embark on a new career. To do that, she knew she needed some additional education, so, at age 38, she enrolled in an advanced degree program at the University of Virginia. She rented an apartment close to the school, and she and Katie started on a new adventure. They developed new routines of their very own that included going for a run first thing in the morning before class, eating breakfast together, then snuggling together on the couch after Randy's long day of learning and Katie's long day of waiting. Throughout the trials of Randy's doctoral program, Katie was there for her, always happy to see her, regardless of her mood or state of exhaustion.

After graduating and building a therapy practice, Randy bought a townhouse, and Randy and Katie moved again. The two of them were their own family and not in need of anyone. In the midst of all this change—divorce, moves, school, career—they had their friendship, their routines, and their favorite games and foods. With Katie by her side, Randy felt as if she could take on the world. Randy's practice thrived, and she soon bought a house with a yard, decorated it, and planted a garden. Katie loved to run in the yard, as this was something she never had before. By all accounts, life was good.

Shortly after the third move, Randy met Bill. He was everything she had ever wanted in a man—caring, compassionate, sensitive, warm, and friendly. Most important, he loved dogs and loved Katie. Randy knew this relationship was special because it felt so right. Never had anyone made her feel so happy about life. She loved Bill not only for who he was but also for who she was when she was with him.

But Katie was jealous. She wasn't used to sharing Randy and was reluctant to let her best friend form this new relationship. After some patience and time, Katie's love and loyalty for Randy transcended to Bill, and soon they were living together harmoniously. And then, just when the new family had bonded, the unthinkable occurred. Bill and Randy went away for the weekend, and they arranged for a dog sitter they had used in the past to care for Katie. Although usually fine with exercising in the enclosed yard, this time Katie jumped the backyard fence and headed off to explore the neighborhood. As she was crossing a street, a car came speeding around the corner. The driver didn't see Katie and ran over her. Katie died instantly.

Randy was in shock over her beloved Katie's death. In her heart, Katie was permanent, and Randy was unprepared emotionally for Katie to leave. They had been through so much together that her death punctured any other grief she had ever experienced.

Looking back, Randy can see how vital Katie was through four major life transitions: divorce, return to school, establishing a career, and building a healthy relationship. Katie was the one stable part of her life during all the turmoil. Randy believes it was as if Katie's life cycle followed her through the destruction of what she had to leave behind in order to give birth to a new life. Though Randy was heartbroken to lose her, she was and still is grateful for Katie's presence and love during those years. Through her life and her death, Katie taught Randy about love and letting go.

Completing the Circle

UNDERSTANDING THE circle of life and its inherent transitions is a challenge for all ages, particularly for children. Teaching our children about these various life stages can be stressful. Fortunately, our companion animals can help us make sense of change and give us support and love while we face any situation. If handled poorly, these transitions can drag us down, causing us to waste years caught in fear and despair. If handled well, they can help us grow to love ourselves and feel hope for the future. In the end, it's what we learn from life's transitions and how we apply the learning that counts.

The circle of life is a difficult concept to understand logically, and regardless of the amount of energy we devote to studying it, there will always be things we simply cannot comprehend. The only thing we understand for certain is that some of life's mysteries are sweet and others painful. However, I believe in the magic that life's mysteries can bring, for without some unanswered questions, life would quickly get boring. Think about it. How exciting would life be if we knew our destiny with absolute certainty or if we understood the meaning of life? Where would the adventure be? What would there be left to discover, to get excited about?

While we may never learn the absolute truths we seek, we can gain the peace of mind that comes from knowing we are not alone in our experiences and that we can rely on our companion animals for the support we need. By observing the life cycles of our pets, we get a glimpse into our own mortality and all the wonders life has to offer.

PET LESSON #3:

THE CIRCLES OF LIFE

Exercises: How to Use This Pet Lesson in Your Everyday Life

1. Think back to a transition in your life. Did you have a companion animal at your side? If not, has a pet supported a friend or family member through a major life transition? What did you/they learn? How can you apply that wisdom during new transitions in your life?

2. Are there children in your life who could learn more about life and death from the presence of a companion animal? Or whose social development might benefit from interacting with a pet? How will you support their learning and incorporate the lessons into their daily life?

3. Imagine a dear pet from the past being at your side as you go through a difficult or transitional time in your life. How would your companion animal support you now? What can you learn from applying this insight to your life presently? How can you benefit from this observation in the future?

4. Like Paula, have you had to leave a piece of yourself behind during a time of loss in your life? Feel the spirit of your companion animal surrounding you. Let your beloved pet's love help you to know that you are whole and that nothing is missing.

5. Michael and David learned about birth and death from their pets. Are there some more subtle life transitions that you were not conscious of in the past that you are aware of now? Notice what you've learned over time. How can you apply this observation to your life today?

6. Similar to how Randy handled the death of her dog, Katie, try to look past your grief over a pet's death or some other ending and see it as an opportunity for rebirth. How can this ending be a beginning for you?

CHAPTER FOUR

Lessons of Developing Our Instincts

"Without many inborn instincts to guide us, we as human beings need models for how to live. We need a sense of our own possibilities and limits, and we find them not only in the artificial rules and restraints imposed by human society but in the lessons for living suggested by biology and by the earth itself. In a fundamental way, we need other creatures to tell us who we are."

—GARY KOWALSKI, *The Souls of Animals*

GUT FEELINGS ... intuition ... following your heart— all describe the natural instincts we each have yet often ignore. Our instincts are inherent and are meant to protect us from harm. Have you ever gotten a "funny feeling" after meeting someone? Have you ever found your way out of an undesirable location even though you've never been there before? Have you ever chosen to do something just because it "felt right?" If so, you let your instincts take over and guide your actions.

Animals live by their instincts every day. Whether they're hunting field mice or alerting their human companions to visitors, they're doing what feels right and listening to their internal programming. Our companion animals don't second-guess their actions. They seem to react to situations intuitively, and their first instincts are usually right on target.

As our culture has evolved and become more high-tech, many people have forgotten how to listen to their instincts. They jump into and out of relationships abruptly, change jobs haphazardly, and take unnecessary risks without regard to what their internal safety mechanisms are telling them. When reflecting on the situation, these same people will say, "I should have listened to my gut," "I should have known better," or "I had a feeling things would turn out like this." While it's always easier to speculate on an event after it has transpired, poor outcomes can often be avoided, or at least lessened, when we trust ourselves and follow the wisdom that's inherent in each of us.

When we observe the instinctive nature our companion animals display, we learn how vital following our instincts is for our survival and growth. By opening our minds to what our "heart" tells us, we can take the steps necessary to reconnect with our intuitive spirit. When we listen to our instincts, we live a life more in harmony with our natural inclinations, and we often make better decisions.

The Power to Trust

Samantha, or Sammie, as everyone called her, had been a Best Friends Animal Sanctuary dog all her life. An 11-year-old golden–Chesapeake Bay retriever mix, she was a "hider"—when people would walk by looking for a dog to adopt, Sammie would run and hide underneath one of the benches in her compound. As a result, she was always passed over.

In May 1999, a fire broke out at the sanctuary. Many of the dogs' homes, including Sammie's, were engulfed in smoke and flames. The volunteers on duty that day worked diligently to get all the animals out safely. They braved the heat and smoke and ran into the blaze multiple times, carrying and herding out as many animals as possible each time. After all the animals were safely out, one volunteer ran back into the fire for one last look—he wanted to be certain no animals were still inside. When he did, Sammie, possibly trying to protect his home, followed the volunteer back in. A staff member who saw Sammie returning to the building ran in after her.

The thick smoke blinded him and made it nearly impossible to see where Sammie went. The staff member crouched down on all fours and searched the building, room by room. He finally found Sammie—hiding under a bench. The staff member, who suffered burns as a result of the rescue, pulled Sammie out and brought her for immediate medical attention. Sammie's eyes were damaged beyond repair and had to be removed.

Two months later, Best Friends was hosting a seminar on humane education. Deborah, a lifelong animal lover, traveled from her home in Ohio to Best Friends to attend. Because she had always liked senior dogs and wanted to start a senior dog rescue program one day, she spent most of her free time at Old Friends, the senior section, where they had 60 older dogs. That's where Deborah met Sammie.

When Deborah first saw Sammie, the dog had just been released back into the general population after the fire. She was now in Old Dogs. Deborah had never been around a blind dog before, let alone one who had so recently lost her sight. She was fascinated with Sammie's movements—the way she'd "high-step" her way to her water bowl and out the door. Even though the dog could no longer see, she seemed to sense her surroundings and was able to get along with minimal assistance.

Deborah ended up volunteering at Best Friends for three days, and she spent most of her time with Sammie. Deborah would take her out for daily walks and sit on the porch with her, talking to her and brushing her golden fur. The more time she spent with Sammie, the deeper she fell in love with her. By the time Deborah's visit came to an end, she knew she didn't want to leave without Sammie. Although she couldn't take Sammie home with her that day, she made arrangements to have her flown the very next week from Utah to Ohio.

The day Deborah picked Sammie up from the airport was hot, and Sammie was tired from the journey. During the entire car ride to her new home, Sammie was calm and seemed happy. Deborah had been prepared for the car ride to upset Sammie, but the dog somehow knew that she was going to a good place and that there was nothing to fear. When Sammie arrived at her new home, she was a little reluctant to get out of her crate. Once out, however, she started high-stepping around the yard. She was using her sense of touch to get to know her new territory. Deborah led Sammie inside, where she performed the same ritual to get acquainted with her new home. What amazed Deborah the most was that even though Sammie had never lived in a home, never flown in an airplane, and never ridden in a car, this dog, who had just lost her sight, handled each situation with ease and adapted quickly. She seemed to know the importance of letting her instincts guide her through every new adventure.

Within two weeks, it was as if Sammie had lived with Deborah all her life. She knew where her food and water bowls were, how to get outside using the ramp Deborah had built for her, and how to get along with the other two senior dogs Deborah already cared for.

Once in her new home, one of Sammie's favorite activities was to visit the lake near Deborah's house. Although Sammie had never been to a lake before, as soon as she smelled the water, she'd break into a run and make her way to the shoreline. With her head held high, she'd let her nose guide her, leading her around any obstacles in her path. Rocks, trees, people, or other animals were no hindrance for Sammie. Each time they went to the lake, Deborah would watch Sammie with awe. She was always amazed at how Sammie trusted herself and listened to her instincts, knowing that they would keep her out of harm's way.

Deborah had never met an animal who had to rely on her instincts as much as Sammie. She believes that if people would trust themselves and follow their gut the way Sammie did, they would lead more fulfilling and productive lives. "There's an old adage that 'blind dogs see with their heart,'" Deborah says. "Sammie taught me the importance of listening to my heart and trusting myself to make the right choices. Whenever I have an urge to second-guess myself about a decision, I simply think of Sammie and trust my own judgment." Sammie's trusting her instincts guided Deborah to a new enlightenment that encouraged her to develop her own intuitive nature.

Instinctive Behaviors

"INSTINCT" IS INDEED a complex concept. We each have an instinctive nature, yet we often don't recognize it as such. We call our fears and apprehensions "silly" and "unfounded," when, in reality, our instincts are rearing up, trying to warn us about a situation.

Many people assert that babies have strong instincts. A crying baby in the arms of a stranger often calms down once in mother's arms. We often remark that babies somehow know their parents and can sense when the person holding them is a stranger or someone apprehensive of being in the presence of babies. If this is true, why do we lose this instinct as we age? Why do babies react instinctively to people, and why do adults often suppress their gut feelings?

A Lesson in Discernment

Kellce is a tall, beautiful blonde woman with deep-set brown eyes and a trim yet shapely figure. Unlike "beautiful people" who seem to separate themselves from others, Kellce always went out of her way to put everyone she met at ease. It was important to Kellce that others felt comfortable around her, and because of that, she developed a knack for making people of all ages laugh. Focusing on the other person's comfort first was an old habit that she never questioned—until Thor came into her life.

Thor is a mountain of a dog, a gentle giant with keenly attuned instincts. He is a white Great Pyrenees and towers over most dogs. Thor has lived with Kellce and her husband, Steve, for the past nine years. In that time, he has taken on the role of family protector with dignity and commitment. Kellce in particular has learned a lot from Thor's strong presence and his ability to follow his instincts about people and situations.

Kellce asserts that Thor studies those he is around and has the ability to read body language. Thor normally doesn't bark at people, so when he does, Kellce pays attention. One time when Kellce and her husband needed their broken air-conditioner repaired, Thor couldn't contain himself around the repairman. His bark thundered throughout the house. The repairman concluded that the couple needed a new air-conditioner. It was mid-July in the South, and the temptation to pay the $1,500 necessary to replace the unit was overwhelming. However, Thor's response got Kellce feeling "funny" about the man and his estimate. She contacted another repair shop for a second opinion. As it turned out, the problem was a broken part that cost $100 to replace.

Thor's keen instincts have proved useful on other occasions as well. As customer service consultants, Kellce and Steve travel a lot for business, and several years ago they decided to take Thor on trips with them whenever possible. One time, while traveling in Texas, they met a woman by the hotel pool. She was friendly and talkative and kept trying to pet Thor. Kellce noticed that Thor avoided the woman's touch. The woman reached for Thor in order to finger his coat, but he skillfully moved around Kellce, stepping over his leash to avoid the woman. Shocked at Thor's behavior, the woman said she was a vet tech and that animals usually "love me." She told Kellce that she couldn't figure out what was wrong with Thor.

Later on, after Kellce and Steve were going to dinner and Thor was settled in the room, Kellce noticed that the woman was still by the pool and appeared very drunk. As she got closer, Kellce noticed that the woman's face was bruised. Kellce checked with the front desk to ask about the woman. The receptionist replied, "Stay away from her; she's bad news. She comes here for happy hour and tries to mooch off people. We ask her to leave, and she just keeps returning. Now we're concerned because she claims that she fell and hurt herself due to a loose board on our pool deck."

"Thor is discretionary in his protectiveness and in his approach to other living creatures," Kellce observes. "He taught me that dignity is important, and that if you give your enthusiasm away too freely, you aren't really assessing the situation. You're using the same approach with all people rather than using your instincts to distinguish their differences."

Learning from Thor's reliance on his instincts and looking for nonverbal clues has helped Kellce assess situations better. She is now less likely to jump in to make others feel at home, instead waiting until she "gets a feel for the person and the surroundings." She uses Thor's "watch and learn" technique to take note of unfamiliar environments and to watch for potentially unsafe situations, and it has served her well in her travels and on home turf. In the past she may not have noticed if someone was following her; now she's pretty sure she would. Thor helped Kellce fine-tune her instincts—today she's observant of the world around her and uses her intuition to keep trouble at bay.

The Origins of Instinct

BEING IN THE PRESENCE of animals can increase our self-awareness and help us be more in tune with our environment. In the case of Kellce and Thor, Kellce learned more about her tendency to be so concerned about others' comfort that she wasn't always in touch with her gut feelings about a person or a situation. Thor helped her reconnect with her instincts.

What is instinct? Instinct involves the innate programming present in all animals that enables us to respond adaptively to a variety of situations in our environment. Some researchers have made the distinction between behaviors that are learned and behaviors that are instinctive, such as responses involving feeding, mating, and aggression. These distinctions have become blurred because learned behaviors and instinctive behaviors interact to guide an animal's behavior in appropriate ways.[1]

Look at maternal behavior in female dogs, for example. A female dog instinctively knows how to feed and care for her pups, of course. But what about caring for another species? There have been cases of dogs serving as surrogate mothers for other species, such as cats. Is this is an example of purely instinctive behavior, or is it instinctive behavior in one situation (with their own pups) and learned behavior in another (with the kittens)? Human behavior is no different. We respond to situations with our instincts as well as our intellect.

The Heart of Instinct

IN HIS BOOK, *How to Know God,* Deepak Chopra tells a story about how following his instinct led to his saving both his and his daughter's lives. When he was a young medical student, Deepak was studying for an exam and watching his six-month-old daughter. A loud pounding on the door disrupted his quiet. Someone had kicked in the front door and was in his apartment.

Within moments, a large, menacing man stood in front of Deepak. In his right hand, the stranger was holding a baseball bat, and his eyes and body language communicated danger. Deepak saw himself as a nonviolent person and the thought of physically harming another was not part of his belief system. However, in this instance, instinct took over. Deepak quickly grabbed the bat from the man's hand and hit him hard on the head. As the man lay in his own blood on the floor, Deepak called the police.

Moments later the police arrived and took the intruder away. When the police ran a background check on him, they discovered that the man had several prior assault charges against him and was a suspect for murder. By being present in the moment, it appears that Deepak acted on his natural instincts in a way that was totally different than he might of anticipated.

In the following story, Kate also wound up protecting her young in a way she couldn't have anticipated when, one Saturday morning, she and her two cats, Sasha and Tara, had the adventure of a lifetime.

A Howling Encounter

Kate is an organizational development consultant who built her home in south-central Colorado, in a spectacularly beautiful high mountain desert valley. The small community there shared Kate's love of the wilderness, protecting the rights of its wild animals, even if that stewardship came at the expense of the humans encroaching on this same wilderness.

Kate lived alone and resisted having a companion animal. While she had always loved animals and had been quite close to her family pets when she was young, as an adult Kate didn't want her freedom hampered by the needs of a companion animal. One day, however, a friend surprised her with the gift of a little kitten. At first she was quite uneasy, since cats behave so differently from the cuddly, obedient dogs she had known and trained as a child. And since her childhood allergies had prevented her from being around cats, having a cat was the last thing she ever expected in her life. Yet here she was, with a gift she couldn't refuse.

Three-month-old Tara was a beautiful longhaired tortoise-colored Maine coon combination. Tara's gold eyes and the way she marched into a room with her full tail erect evoked royalty. The white markings on Tara's face gave her the countenance of a wise owl. Kate grew really close to Tara, and she hated leaving Tara alone when she was working and traveling.

On Independence Day 1998, Kate woke up with the decision to adopt another kitten so Tara would have a playmate. That very afternoon, Kate walked into the annual celebration in the park. There, under a huge old cottonwood tree, friends of hers were giving away kittens from a large cardboard box. The couple had taken in a wild, pregnant cat, offering refuge to her and her soon-to-be-born babies. They described Sasha as "the pick of the litter."

Sasha was "the first out of the womb, the first to open her eyes, and the most agile of the litter." A sleek and compact, shorthaired, tabby-and-tortoise-shell combination, Sasha was auburn and brown and had sensitive green eyes. She was the most distinctive looking of her half a dozen, all-gray brothers and sisters. "She looks more like a tree squirrel than a cat," her vet once remarked. This little Independence Day kitty moved about with the graceful motions of a wild jungle cat. She lived up to the image—Sasha loved to hunt and stalk her prey, and she did so with the independence she exhibited on the very day she arrived in Kate's life.

One morning, two summers later, Kate jumped out of bed early to work on the computer. She sat upstairs in her office, enjoying working at home, comfortable in her floral Japanese robe and lightweight slippers. Tara was at the window near her, looking out from their second-floor perspective. After working for several hours, Kate noticed that Tara was suddenly moving erratically, frantically pacing the windowsill and letting out yelps to get Kate's attention. In the same instant, Kate heard a blood-curdling scream from outside. She immediately knew the scream was Sasha's.

Without even looking out the window, Kate instinctively ran down the stairs and out the front door onto the cactus and other prickly plant life that surrounds her desert home. She might as well have been barefoot for all the protection her flimsy summer slippers provided. But Kate didn't care. Her feet could be bloody. She had to protect her kitty. "I became total instinct," says Kate. Running onto her driveway, she came face-to-face with a coyote that was gripping Sasha in its mouth and about to turn and run off with her. From the pit of her stomach, Kate screamed more intensely than she ever had in her life. Kate's cry so stunned the coyote that it dropped Sasha from its mouth.

Kate then chased the coyote off her land, although the animal didn't make it easy. It would run, then stop and look back at her, as if it couldn't believe its eyes and was going to give it another try. Kate continued to run after it until it crossed the road away from her home. Upon returning, Kate gathered up the stunned cat, tenderly avoiding her wounds and worrying about the eye that wouldn't open. She drove Sasha directly to the vet, an hour away. The coyote's sharp teeth had punctured Sasha in her back and stomach and just above her left eye. The vet treated Sasha's injuries topically and gave Kate antibiotics and eye cream to administer for one week. It was too soon to know whether Kate's beautiful, wild pet had suffered internal injuries or whether her eye would recover.

Miraculously, Sasha recovered within a week. Today she is back home and continues hunting near the house. When asked why she still lets her cats out after this frightening incident, Kate explains, "At first I decided it was too dangerous to let them out of the house at all. But after a while, I realized that life is dangerous. We can attempt to be prudent with the risks we take, but we can't eliminate risk, no matter what we do or don't do. We can't live a full, healthy life if we attempt to shelter ourselves from life itself. Sasha loves to hunt close to home, and that's part of her wild nature. I can't take that from her without robbing her of that wild essence that I so enjoy about her. What I can do is use common sense about when I let her out, and keep a watchful eye."

Never having had cats before, Kate had to learn from them how to be with them. She couldn't rely on past experience. Being with them has deepened her capacity to nurture as well as her ability to be fully present in each moment, without knowing what that moment may bring. Kate's cats have shown her how to merge presence with instinct.

The Emotional Side of Instinct

TO FOLLOW YOUR INSTINCTS, you must first be self-aware. Those who are self-aware are able to temper their emotions and connect with others in a variety of situations.

It's a subtle form of intuition that is one of the building blocks to "emotional intelligence," a concept popularized by psychologist and writer Daniel Goleman.

According to Goleman, emotional intelligence is a broad-based term that includes self-awareness, managing your emotions effectively, motivation, empathy, reading other people's feelings accurately, and social skills like teamwork, leadership, and managing relationships.[2] When we are aware of these aspects of ourselves, we can sense them in others and react to them appropriately. If we aren't aware of our own emotions, we can't be aware of what others may be experiencing either. This puts us at a serious disadvantage in relating with others, at work, at home, and in friendships.

In the *Harvard Business Review,* Goleman writes about "emotional self-awareness" as the ability "to read and understand your emotions as well as recognize their impact" on yourself and others.[3] Emotional intelligence deals with intuition, or "gut instinct," and the ability to size up a person or situation. Those unable to do this often wind up with their careers and their lives sidetracked. Developing emotional intelligence is an important life skill.

We can learn a lot about emotional intelligence from observing and interacting with our animal companions. Rocky is a prime example of an animal teacher who has taught many to be more self-aware and emotionally intelligent.

A Greater Understanding

Even though Rick was prepared for bad news, the words stunned him and left him temporarily speechless. "You have Parkinson's disease, Rick," stated the doctor. Rick sat in a daze as the doctor explained the disease, his prognosis, and current treatment plans. By the time Rick left the doctor's office, his mind was spinning, and he wondered how he would tell his wife, Sylvia, the news.

That evening, after Sylvia got home from work, Rick sat down with her and told her. Upon hearing the diagnosis,

Sylvia found herself in emotional turmoil. Unfamiliar with the disease, she was scared. Envisioning the worst for the man she loved and had spent the past 45 years with, she was sad—and angry.

Throughout their married life, Rick and Sylvia had kept a wellness perspective to their health. They believed that if they focused on staying well, any disease they contracted would heal naturally. They knew they'd have to take the same approach with Rick's Parkinson's disease. As Rick says, "The Parkinson's diagnosis was difficult to accept. Yet as I think back, I had the signs of this nerve-damaging disability for years. Sylvia and I decided that we needed to read up on all the progressive treatments available."

For the next few months, Rick's focus on the disease was all-consuming. He became obsessed with Parkinson's research and devoted all his energy to it. His needs were his first priority. And while his friends and family understood Rick's sudden obsession, they were not always sure how to support him. He was, in essence, letting the disease take over his life.

During his research, Rick discovered the importance of Parkinson's patients staying physically active. He learned that working out daily would help keep his muscles stimulated so they wouldn't deteriorate. A Parkinson's support group sponsored a workshop on how horseback riding can help. That's when Rick met Edie Dopking, the founder of Quantum Leap Farm in Odessa, Florida. Quantum Leap Farm is a riding stable for the emotionally and physically handicapped. Edie gave a presentation on how horseback riding offers the combination of movement and balance that's beneficial to those with Parkinson's. Rick was intrigued by this concept and immediately made an appointment with Edie for the following week. That's when he met Rocky for the first time.

Rick admits that when he arrived at Quantum Leap for his first ride, he was still a bit skeptical. He understood from his research how horseback riding could help, but he didn't see the value in a real-life horse. As he remembers, "My attitude was that I might as well ride a mechanical horse if that's all that was necessary to help my condition."

Edie was present for Rick's first ride. She recalls, "Rick was all over the horse when he first came to see us. Because of leg weakness, he couldn't keep balanced. Good thing he was on Rocky, our most sensitive and instinctive horse. It's as if Rocky has an intuition about the disabled. He knows how to take the lead with a real gentleness and can follow the rider's lead, too."

An Appaloosa horse with rose-gray coloring and white-and-chocolate-like flecks all over, Rocky stands about four foot ten. He gets his name from Rocky Road ice cream, as his coat seems to have all the same colors.

Rick was immediately impressed with Rocky. As Rick rode, the horse was able to discriminate between Rick's unpredictable bodily responses and real commands. Since this was Rick's first ride, in the beginning one person would walk the horse, taking the lead, and there would be two "side-walkers," on the left and right sides of the horse, holding Rick in place. Rocky's sensitivity to Rick and his ability to skillfully balance with Rick's erratic movements caught Rick's attention. "I realized that Rocky had a distinct personality and that he had feelings," says Rick. He believes it was Rocky's attunement to him that showed him that Rocky was so much more than a "barnyard animal." "I had never bonded with animals before," Rick says. "Rocky and I have developed a real affection. Interacting with him is a true act of love."

As Rick became aware of all Rocky was doing, he also started to see the additional help those around him were giving. He slowly started taking the focus off himself and his disease, and he began seeing all the people who were helping him in his struggle. Being with Rocky reminded Rick that there were a lot of people around him doing all they could to help. His self-absorption over the previous few years had kept him from seeing this. "Because of Rocky's example, I began to thank the lead and side-walkers as well as Rocky after each ride. I became more aware of those around me and less self-focused." Rocky's presence in Rick's life helped Rick develop his emotional intelligence and improve his ability to relate to others.

In recognition of his hard work and impact on people's lives, Rocky recently received the Florida Animal Health Foundation's State Award for Ambassador of the Human–Animal Bond. Today, Rick continues to ride Rocky and other horses. He is able to do so on his own, without the leader or side-walkers. In addition, he and his wife, Sylvia, have created something they call "brainrobics," which is a learning methodology that teaches people how to activate all portions of their brains. This activation leads to improved neurological and mental functioning and can be of great help to those with disabling diseases like Parkinson's. Rick is thankful for the progress he has made with the help of others. "My belief in God, my family's support, and Rocky's able assistance were the major ingredients in managing this disease."

The Gateway to Enlightenment

BEING INSTINCTIVE means trusting yourself and your judgment to do what's right at the appropriate time—even if it goes against the precepts of conventional wisdom and your own opinions. Unfortunately, many of us don't trust ourselves enough to follow our instincts. We allow fear and doubt to keep us from listening to that "inner voice" that speaks to each of us when we're self-aware. When we ignore our internal inclinations or fail to respond to what our hearts tell us, we deny ourselves the very essence of our humanity.

We also risk the chance of being out of tune with people, animals, and all living things around us. This emotionally unintelligent behavior has implications for our own development and the welfare of others.

By observing the instinctive nature of animals, we can reconnect with that inherent part of ourselves. At the same time, we can discover aspects of our personality that we didn't know were there. We can tap into some basic emotions, like empathy, fear, and happiness, and gain the strength to act in positive ways we never dreamed possible. As we learn the importance of ignoring self-doubt and reap the rewards that come with following our instincts, we increase our awareness and forge deeper relationships with those around us.

PET LESSON #4:

LESSONS OF DEVELOPING OUR INSTINCTS

Exercises: How to Use This Pet Lesson in Your Everyday Life

1. Try walking in your environment sightless. Find a friend or family member to blindfold you and guide you throughout your home. Think about Sammie while you're doing this. When finished, talk about how you felt. Were you able to trust your instincts to guide you in unfamiliar territory? If not, what kept you from trusting yourself?

2. Make a special effort to observe the people and events around you. Like Thor, use a "watch and learn" technique to discern the nuances of each situation.

3. Have you ever surprised yourself by reacting out of total instinct like Kate did? What did you learn?

4. On a scale of 1 through 5, with 1 being not at all developed and 5 being fully developed, how would you rate your own emotional intelligence, especially self-awareness and your social skills? Why? If your score is low, what are some ways you can improve it?

5. Part of being emotionally attuned to others is being patient, like Rocky. Think of a situation where you are normally impatient. Ask yourself how you can be more attuned and responsive the next time you are in that situation.

CHAPTER FIVE

Lessons of Healing

"A true friend walks in when the rest of the world walks out."

—UNKNOWN

BEING SICK can be frightening. While medical doctors and biologists may be able to approach sickness from a scientific standpoint, the rest of us often let our emotions take over during times of illness, often our negative emotions. It's easy to become scared, depressed, or pessimistic. Even when we know a positive attitude is vital to any remedy, when an illness is life threatening, hopelessness can set in, making our condition worse.

It's during these times of wavering health—whether it's the flu or a catastrophic illness—that we seek out others for help and solace. Although we know there's little our friends and family can do for us physically, their emotional support helps us get through and sometimes accept our medical condition.

One of the important life lessons that animals teach us is the power of our presence in helping others heal. Few people can deny feeling helpless around someone who is sick. In fact, we often wonder if "just being there" really does make a difference—maybe we're just in the way. I believe that the presence of another, whether human or animal, does make a difference in the quality of life a sick person experiences.

When loved ones, friends, and companion animals surround us, our spirits lift, and they put us in a more positive mind-set. It's this improved thinking that can begin the healing process. When we can look beyond our illnesses and once again see the joy in life, we begin to heal our souls, which, in turn, can encourage our bodies to heal. People get sick from the inside out, and they heal from the inside out. A positive attitude can help us heal, be more open to treatment options, or, in some cases, gain the will to live. In following the example of our companion animals, we learn that if we stay close to those who are ill and if we are loving and positive, our presence can ease pain, provide support, and foster healing.

A New Desire to Live

DESPITE THE advent of so many medical marvels, people are still getting sick at an alarming rate. With new medications and discoveries, we should be some of the healthiest people in history. The reality, however, is that Americans are spending an astronomical amount on health care costs—more than $750 billion a year, to be exact. Even more startling, that figure is expected to increase 20 percent annually.

As our health continues to deteriorate despite modern science, more and more of us are turning to natural approaches for our health care needs. In the midst of all the holistic remedies, animal-assisted therapy is growing by leaps and bounds. Many people keep a pet for companionship and affection, but current research suggests that interacting with an animal can also help keep people out of the doctor's office or hospital emergency room.

Studies on pet ownership over the last 10 to 15 years have found that companion animals are associated with lowered stress levels, fewer doctors' visits, and higher survival rates after a catastrophic illness. They have also helped psychiatric patients overcome anxiety. Although no one has identified precisely why animals can help comfort the sick and give such positive physiological and psychological benefits, it most likely has something to do with an animal's ability to kindle emotion.

Cotton's Soft Touch

Georgia was a full-spirited woman who had lived independently her entire life. Although her husband had a job that could support the family, Georgia always enjoyed working outside the home, despite the fact that few women of her day did so unless they had to. She simply felt confident knowing that she could make it on her own. She raised her daughter, Merci, to have that same spirit. When Georgia's husband passed away, her self-sufficiency enabled her to support herself.

After her retirement, Georgia worked in her garden and volunteered at the community hospital. She also routinely embarked on solo adventures across the county. Those who knew her called her an "inspiration" because of her free spirit and her love for life.

As time progressed, Georgia began having "spells," during which she suddenly couldn't remember her name or where she was. She would see and hear things that other people could not. Concerned, Merci encouraged her mother to see a doctor. Georgia complied, and after extensive testing, she was diagnosed with dementia.

The doctor's words filled her with fear and apprehension. She was terrified of what the disease would do to her mind, and she was angry that her independence and free spirit would soon be gone. She didn't know what she would do with her life once she was unable to connect with her family and friends. Within months, it became more and more difficult for Georgia to take care of herself and perform basic day-to-day tasks. She seemed to be in her own world and would often get lost in it. It was obvious Georgia could no longer live alone, so she moved in with her daughter and son-in-law and Cotton, the couple's affectionate Lhasa apso.

Merci was surprised to see just how much ground her mom had lost. They couldn't connect any longer, which greatly disturbed Merci because the two always had a close relationship. And Georgia would often see things that existed only in her mind, leaving Merci and her husband confused and nervous. Georgia seemed to be living in a fog. With each passing day, Merci grew more worried about her mother's well-being.

Cotton, too, was getting on in years. At 11 years old, he no longer walked with the energy of a young and healthy dog. He was still a vital part of the family, but between taking care of Georgia and working full time, Merci and her husband just didn't have as much time to spend with Cotton as they used to. Cotton missed being with them—he liked the companionship. And he soon filled the void—with Georgia.

As Georgia and Cotton spent their days together, a bond began to develop. Although Georgia's mind was failing, she still had a lot of energy and would take Cotton on walks. The two would stroll around the neighborhood, with Cotton always leading Georgia back home should she become disoriented during their outing. When Georgia seemed to blank out or slip into a trance, Cotton would jump or bark to get her attention and bring her back to reality.

As winter turned into spring, Cotton and Georgia would sit on the back porch together, enjoying the long lazy days. Cotton would frequently sit on Georgia's lap or sit by her side as she watched television or read. With one utterance of the word "walk," Cotton was at the door, ready to go out with his trusted companion to visit all the nooks and crannies of the neighborhood.

Georgia and Cotton helped each other. In Georgia's presence, Cotton had energy again and was more like his old self. Under Cotton's loving attention, Georgia blossomed. She regained an interest in gardening and was more in tune with her family. Cotton's love and attention helped Georgia function during those fragile years.

"If it were not for Cotton's companionship and presence, Mom would have completely lost touch with the world," declared Merci. "Their friendship brought joy and happiness once again into the life of a woman who has given so much to others."

How Animals Help

ANIMALS HAVE feelings and emotions, just as people do. The truth of this simple statement has been debated for a long time, and its lack of acceptance in professional arenas has had a profound and negative impact on the treatment of animals. Amazingly, that animals have and express emotions has not been fully accepted or researched by the veterinary and medical professions. Dr. Allen Schoen is one who champions the belief that animals have emotions.[1] As Schoen and others report, PET (positron emission tomography) scans, which are frequently used to gauge the brain's response to emotional stimuli, show that emotional states, such as anger, happiness, and fear, indicate similar brain activity in animals and humans. In other words, human and animal emotional states are alike. I believe companion animals and their humans can share emotional states, share feelings, and that this is why they bond at deeper and deeper levels.

Empathy is capturing the feeling and meaning of what someone else is experiencing and conveying back to them that you understand. Feeling understood, knowing someone truly empathizes with us—this is one of the most healing interactions we can experience.[2] In my field of human development and growth, the therapeutic effects of empathy have been documented for some time. It is seen as a vital component in psychotherapy and other treatment programs.[3] In graduate school, I spent countless hours attempting to empathize with other students and later with patients so that I could build trust and communicate that I understood what they were experiencing. It is from this base of trust that healing and change occurs.

Although animals don't communicate with words, they have the ability to convey that they understand when their human companions are sad, sick, or happy. In the hundreds of "animal teaching stories" that I've heard and collected, people usually state that their companion animals seem to know how they're feeling. Pets convey this awareness to us by altering their behavior to fit our emotional states, such as sitting by our sides, licking our hands, or jumping on our laps.

Three-Legged Wonder

Everyone who sees Zeus knows that he is a very special dog. Zeus is a black Labrador–coonhound mix with a birth defect—he is missing his left front leg. Over the years, Zeus and his unstoppable spirit have made many people smile, but the incident that to this day causes Theresa's eyes to grow bright with tears happened when she and Zeus were visiting Washington, D.C.

Theresa and Zeus were strolling down a sidewalk near the grassy Mall enjoying a bright summer day. The air felt crisp and clean, and Theresa remembers thinking that nothing could ruin such a beautiful day. As they continued to walk, she noticed an older man in a wheelchair rolling down the walk toward them. The way the man's pant legs hung from the chair made it obvious that he was missing his lower legs. She heard him muttering to those he passed, but she couldn't make out his precise words. As he got closer, his anger was unmistakable. The old man was cursing and yelling at people to get out of his way. His anger seemed to spring from every pore of his body. "You son-of-a-bitch bastard," he'd scream as he attempted to get by someone in the crowd.

As the man neared Theresa and Zeus, Theresa began stepping to the side to avoid his verbal wrath. But Zeus, on a retractable leash, hopped over to the wheelchair-bound man. The man immediately stopped his wheelchair in its tracks and looked at Zeus for what seemed like an eternity to Theresa but was actually only a few seconds. The man soon broke out in a big, wide smile. When the man started to pet him, Zeus, who had never once jumped on anyone, put his front leg on the man's lap. While the man was smiling and petting Zeus, he said, "You understand, don't you?" Then Zeus hopped off, and the man wheeled away.

As the man continued down the walk, he wasn't cursing or yelling at anyone. In fact, he looked contemplative and somewhat content. When Zeus got back to Theresa, she gave him a huge hug. Theresa believes that Zeus somehow had the ability to curb the man's anger and show him true empathy.

"Most people are affected by Zeus," reveals Theresa. "Many of them pity him." But because Zeus understood what it means to be missing a leg, his presence made that man feel better, at least for a little while.

"I cry every time I think of that man," Theresa admits as she recalls this story. She used the experience to guide her and Zeus into a new direction. Today, Theresa is helping Zeus work toward his certification as a therapy dog so he can help other people begin the healing process. He is too special not to share his gift.

The Healing Presence of Animals

WE CAN LEARN so much about our body's natural healing process when we allow animals to enter our lives during times of illness. An animal's presence can help us connect to our natural healing instincts and trigger the inner spirit that makes fighting an illness more conceivable. For example, research has shown that companion animals have a definite positive physiological effect on heart attack and stroke patients.[4] And a study of the attachment between dogs and people has shown that stroking a dog with whom a companion bond has been established significantly decreases blood pressure over time.[5]

The healing presence of companion animals has been well documented. It is impossible to determine when animals were first used specifically to promote physical and psychological health, but the use of horseback riding for people with serious disabilities has been reported for centuries. And as far back as 1792, there is documentation that animals were incorporated into the treatment of mental patients: In attempting to reduce the use of drugs and restraints, the York Retreat in England added animals as part of a forward-thinking approach for treatment.

As far as the United States is concerned, the first suggested use of animals in a therapeutic setting was in 1919 at St. Elizabeth's Hospital in Washington, D.C. There, dogs first served as companions for the psychiatric hospital's resident patients. Following this, the earliest extensive use of companion animals in the United States occurred from 1944 to 1945 at an Army Air Corps convalescent hospital in Pawling, New York. The hospital used the hogs, cattle, horses, and chickens at the hospital's farm in some treatment programs, and patients who interacted with the animals had a higher recovery rate from war experiences. After the war, various hospitals used animals from time to time to aid patients in outpatient psychotherapy. But it wasn't until the 1970s that case studies of animals facilitating therapy with children and senior citizens were reported in any quantity.

More recent studies have been done on the effects of companion animals on HIV patients, chronic schizophrenics, the elderly, coronary patients, and the physically disabled. The results in all instances have been impressive. For example, a study that measured the one-year survival rate of 92 patients discharged from a coronary care unit reported that the overall one-year survival rate was 84 percent—78 of the 92 patients were alive one year after their hospital admission. Fifty-eight percent of the subjects had one or more companion animals. Of the 53 patients who were pet owners, only three (6 percent) died within one year. Of the 39 patients who did not own pets, 11 (28 percent) died. The study further showed that the relationship between pet ownership and survival did not depend on the sex or physiological status of the patient.[6]

Additional studies conducted by Dr. Judith Siegel from the University of California, Los Angeles, found that elderly people who had animal companions needed fewer visits to a doctor.[7] For the general population, she reported that people without pets averaged 9.49 visits to the doctor in one year, while pet owners averaged only 8.42 visits.[8]

In one of the largest studies of its kind, Australian researchers reported that among more than 5,700 volunteers, people with companion animals had lower blood pressure and lower levels of triglycerides (a fat that contributes to heart disease) than those without pets. The differences persisted even when the researchers adjusted for differences in smoking habits, diet, body mass index, and income.[9] In addition to the apparent physiological benefits, companion animals can offer tremendous psychological support to young and old alike. Very often, animals act as social catalysts, forging positive links between people and creating a widening circle of warmth and approval. It is believed this happens because animals provide people with a special kind of nonthreatening, nonjudgmental affection that helps break the cycles of loneliness, helplessness, and social withdrawal.[10]

Very often, our interactions with animals can change the nature of our interactions with other people. Some people have even called animals "social lubricants" because they increase the quantity and quality of social interactions.

Blossom from Within

Whenever Rosemari walks outside and asks, "Where are my babies?" 20 or so squirrels suddenly appear. They scamper down trees and sit around her, patiently waiting for her love and food. Some will proceed to walk on her arms, shoulders, and neck. Rosemari pets and feeds the squirrels regularly and swears they know their names. "I've named all of them," she explains. "If I call out, 'Bo!' the correct squirrel will come to me. I've given them all southern names like that."

One of Rosemari's friends has a daughter, Joanne, who did not speak until she was nine years old. When she started talking, she would speak sparingly, and only to her family. Doctors said there was no medical reason for her not to speak. They suspected it was something psychological and that she would talk more openly in her own due time.

Joanne and her mother were visiting Rosemari one day when Rosemari asked, "Have you ever touched a squirrel?" Joanne shook her head no. Rosemari then motioned for Joanne to follow her outside. Joanne said nothing as they walked outside together.

Once outside, Rosemari called "her babies," and they all came on cue. Suddenly, 20 squirrels were scampering around Rosemari and Joanne. Rosemari proceeded to feed them, and she asked Joanne to help. As the squirrels climbed onto Joanne and ate food right out of her hand,

Joanne could not conceal her delight. She began to laugh and giggle, and she immediately blurted out, "How did you get them to do this? How long will they stay? Can we play with them all afternoon?" For the first time ever, it was hard to keep Joanne quiet.

Joanne began visiting Rosemari on a daily basis, each time talking more and showing greater interest in the squirrels. Soon, the two became friends. The squirrels gave Joanne the much-needed opportunity to have conversations with someone outside her family. Although she is still shy today, Joanne has been able to make friends, and she now communicates well and regularly. Her mother believes that Joanne's discussions with the squirrels opened her up and showed her that social interactions are not as difficult or scary as she might have imagined them to be.

Pets and the Elderly

CURRENT RESEARCH indicates that animals provide the elderly with entertainment, friendship, and a sense of security. They also promote feelings of youthfulness and joy. And one of the main benefits of animal companionship for elderly people is increased activity and mobility. For example, a sedentary senior may be enticed to walk with a dog companion. This increases flexibility, strength, and endurance.[11] In addition, as the older person gets out of the house, he or she can come in contact with others and begin to forge relationships with people again. Having social relationships is a vital component of overall longevity—in a community health study involving 2,754 adult men and women, House, Robbins, and Metzner discovered that individuals reporting higher levels of social relationships were significantly less likely to die during the study's follow-up period.[12]

Rejoining the World

Leocadia was all alone. She had outlived most of her relatives, and she barely knew those who remained. Her friends had passed on, too, and she had no one to call or visit when she got lonely. She socialized less and less over the years, and her depression drove her to eventually become a recluse. She refused to step foot outside her house and opened her door only to get the mail. She made arrangements to have her groceries and other necessities delivered to her.

One day when Leocadia opened the door to get the mail, she noticed a small black-and-white mixed-breed dog. She immediately shooed the dog away, and it ran into the bushes. Leocadia thought the dog was gone for good, but after she went inside, the dog came back and began scratching at her door. Leocadia ignored it.

The dog refused to leave and scratched more frantically than before, yet Leocadia refused to open her door again. Despite Leocadia's insistence that the dog leave, it stayed outside her door for several days, all the while scratching at the door occasionally and barking for attention. It was obvious that the dog was determined to somehow get in. Leocadia began to feel sorry for the animal. She was sure it must be hungry and thirsty, as it was very skinny and panting for water.

Leocadia finally gave in to the poor thing and put some food out. Since she didn't have any dog food in the house, she gave the dog chicken that was left over from the night before and a bowl of water. The dog ate and looked up at her thankfully. The dog spotted the still-open door and immediately walked into the house. Leocadia's first response was to object, but then she stopped. She thought that perhaps the dog's company would be enjoyable. She named the dog Nellie.

Because Leocadia refused to go outside other than to get her mail, the dog was going to have to stay inside, even to go to the bathroom. She placed newspaper on the bathroom floor, and Nellie soon got the idea and became paper-trained. The problem with this arrangement became quickly apparent—the odor.

For the next three weeks, no matter how often she cleaned and disinfected the bathroom, her home had the distinct smell of urine and feces in it. Unable to tolerate the stench any longer, Leocadia tied a rope around Nellie's neck, mustered the courage to walk past her front door, and took Nellie outside. At first they stayed in her front yard and never ventured beyond the property line. Nellie, however, wanted to walk around the rest of the neighborhood. She would pull on her rope to try to get Leocadia to go beyond the property line, but Leocadia held her ground.

Finally one day, after a month of staying in the front yard, Leocadia gave in to Nellie's pulling, and they ventured down the block. As she walked with Nellie, neighbors stopped her and asked her what had happened—they wanted to know why they hadn't seen her in such a long time. She realized that her neighbors truly cared for her. She began conversing with her neighbors and realized that she enjoyed these interactions. All her years of keeping to herself had made her forget how pleasant interacting with others could be. When Nellie came into her life, life for Leocadia once again had purpose.

The Benefits of Involvement

THANKS TO SOME of the research projects involving animal assisted therapy (AAT), many organizations are taking notice of the beneficial effects companion animals have on human health. Typically, trained professionals administer AAT, and the animals involved have to meet certain criteria to be part of the team. Because of the indisputable positive effects companion animals have on the elderly, many influential organizations are getting involved. For instance, the Ralston Purina Company, in conjunction with 350 participating animal shelters across the country, provides elderly people with selected companion animals. Since its inception, the Purina Pets for People program has donated more than $12 million to participating humane shelters and matched more than 100,000 shelter animals with owners. As part of the program, Ralston Purina helps cover the cost of adoption fees, spaying or neutering, an initial veterinary visit, vaccinations, and a Purina Starter Kit. People aged 60 or older can become participants through local humane society organizations.

An organization in California, Canine Companions for Independence, offers trained, adult dogs to serve as arms, legs, and ears for people of all ages who have disabilities. These dogs assist people by pulling wheelchairs, retrieving dropped items, and switching lights on and off. In addition to providing basic assistance, the animals help by giving people an immeasurable amount of love and companionship, which helps boost their morale and their self-esteem. Thanks to these animals, their human companion can regain a sense of independence and self-respect, both instrumental to their healing process.

However, an animal's assistance with the elderly need not be so hands-on. Sometimes just having a companion animal by our side during an illness can give more comfort than words alone.

A Light in the Darkness

All his life, Bill relied on his sharp mind to get ahead. A successful gemologist who owned his own jewelry store, Bill's keen business sense guided him and made him a profitable business owner. People in the community always looked to him for business advice, and they respected his dedication to his craft.

At Bill's side was his cat, Nugget, on whom he often relied for support. Nugget was an abandoned, abused kitten he inherited from some relatives who found the cat but didn't feel like they could keep him. Much to his wife's disapproval, Bill took in the fluffy orange-and-white kitten and named him Nugget.

Over the years, Bill provided the cat with all the love and attention he had. In return, Nugget was Bill's loyal companion. He was the first one to greet Bill every morning, as he would lie on the bed next to Bill and lick his face. When Bill came home from work, Nugget would jump around the house, as if celebrating his best friend's return. At night, after Bill and his wife said goodnight to each other, Nugget would nuzzle with Bill until they both fell asleep.

As Bill entered his 60s, however, he began "forgetting" common things: people's names, his address, the day of the week, and more. At the urging of his family, he went to the doctor. After some tests, the doctor gave him the diagnosis he was dreading: Alzheimer's disease. Bill and his family were devastated. They wondered how someone so smart and mentally sharp could fall prey to such a debilitating illness. They questioned the fairness of life. Most of all, they questioned themselves and how they would handle Bill as his disease progressed. They reached out to each other and vowed they would get through the ordeal together.

Within a year of Bill's diagnosis, his memory began fading more and more. He could no longer remember where he lived or even the fact that he was once a successful gemologist. By the two-year mark, Bill could recognize only a few people in his life. As he went deeper into his mental abyss, he'd often sit with his cat, stroking its fur, and relieving the tension his illness brought on.

The family agreed that it was becoming increasingly more difficult to care for Bill at home. They gathered together to discuss their options. After much deliberation, they agreed that admitting Bill to a skilled nursing facility would be the best option. The family visited several nursing homes and decided to place Bill in one close to home. This arrangement worked out well, as it allowed Bill's wife to visit daily and to take him home for regular outings.

Soon, Bill did not recognize anyone in the family—except Nugget. Whenever he saw the cat, he'd pick him up, and they'd sit together on the porch for hours, with Bill petting his cat's fur and always looking relaxed and content. Nugget never left his lap and always seemed to give Bill the unconditional love and comfort he needed.

It became apparent to everyone that Nugget was Bill's strength and his only remaining connection with his past. Although it pained Bill's wife that he no longer knew who she was, she found comfort in Nugget's being able to bring a spark of life back into Bill's eye. With Bill's memory almost completely gone, Nugget was his only source of comfort in an unfamiliar world.

The Healing Touch

HOW DOES A companion animal assist in healing or in easing discomfort or fear? I believe it has a lot to do with the empathy, respect, unconditional acceptance, and love that animals display. Having these needs met, combined with the simple act of reaching out and touching another living creature, helps put people in the proper emotional state for the healing process to take place.

The act of touching has been observed in several research studies. One study found that being touched and talked to by another person reduced blood pressure and heart rate. Even in a busy hospital setting with mechanical devices and breathing apparatuses hooked up to a patient, the simple touch of a nurse's hand could ease a patient and decrease the frequency of arrhythmia.[13]

Similar healing effects come from physical contact with animals as well. The study mentioned in the previous paragraph also revealed that when people touched or talked to their animals, their blood pressure was significantly lower than when they talked to another person, and sometimes it even was lower than their resting level. Robin and ten Bensel conclude that when people speak with other people, blood pressure has a tendency to go up, but when people interact with animals, their blood pressure is lower.[14] Other researchers have noted that interacting with animals, even just watching them, is pleasurable and relaxing and that it helps people focus on something other than their illness.

A Kindred Connection

Joe was in the twilight of his life and suffered from Alzheimer's. He lived in a nursing home. He couldn't communicate coherently, and he spent most of his days lying in bed or sitting and staring into a corner.

One day, when Ileana Berger, an AAT therapist, and her golden retriever, Sasha, arrived at the nursing home where Joe lived, they walked past the dining room and heard beautiful music. The melodic sound of a piano concerto filled the air. Ileana stood there, amazed at how smoothly and effortlessly the music flowed. The sound enveloped her and made her feel like she was walking on air.

Curious to know who was playing such heartfelt and beautiful music, Ileana opened the door and saw Joe at the piano. She sat and listened without making a sound. When Joe was finished, she smiled and applauded. Joe then patted Sasha lovingly. This began a special communication between the three that had not existed before.

From that day on, whenever Ileana and Sasha visited the nursing home, they made a special stop at Joe's room. Joe was clearly drawn to Sasha's presence, and Sasha's wagging tail made it obvious that she was glad to be with him as well.

Sasha had attended many animal therapy sessions with Ileana. During those visits, Sasha never kissed anyone, but in time, Joe became the exception. Whenever Sasha was with Joe, Joe's face would light up, and he would smile and babble at her. Sasha would reciprocate by bathing his face with kisses. Joe, who never responded to anyone in the nursing home, willingly interacted with Sasha and communicated with her as best he could.

One day when Ileana and Sasha arrived, the nurse on duty said that Joe was dying. His major organs were failing, and he was no longer responding to any of his medications. They immediately went to his room. The staff warned them that Joe wouldn't recognize anyone, but they were wrong.

Sasha went to Joe's side and licked his hand. With that, Joe opened his eyes, stretched out his hand, and lovingly patted Sasha. Then he looked up at Ileana and smiled as if to say, "Thank you for the gift of Sasha." Even though Joe died the next day, having Sasha in his life—something to touch and love—made the loneliness and isolation of Alzheimer's more bearable.

One of the beautiful aspects of AAT is that it knows no boundaries. Children as well as adults can benefit from the healing effects an animal helps stimulate. AAT therapist Pam Dickens works with a lot of sick children. She vividly recalls a young patient who was particularly touched by the animals.

The Comforting Kiss

Five-year-old Jordan had brain cancer. Because of the severity of his condition, he was admitted to the children's hospital as a long-term patient. Unlike most five-year-olds, whose days consist of playing with friends and watching cartoons, Jordan's days were filled with medical tests and painful treatments. On a weekly basis, however, Jordan would escape the doctor's poking and prodding and visit Zeus the Moose, a large Labrador mix Pam brought to therapy sessions.

Jordan's chemotherapy sessions often left him feeling quite ill. Nausea and fatigue were his most common side effects. Whenever Jordan felt sick from his treatments, he'd sit with Zeus the Moose for the comfort he needed. By simply hugging and petting the dog, he could get into a better frame of mind and return to his usual happy-go-lucky self.

Jordan's parents would not allow him to have a dog of his own. They thought he was too young to handle such a large responsibility, and they wanted him to wait until his cancer went into remission before bringing a pet into his life. When the doctors told his parents that Jordan's cancer was terminal, they changed their mind. They wanted to give their son everything they could to make his short life as happy as possible.

Jordan accompanied his parents to the local humane society. All the dogs were eager to see them, and as they jumped in their kennel runs, they seemed to be shouting, "Pick me! Pick me!" Jordan was immediately drawn to a small black terrier mix dog. His parents agreed, and they adopted him. Jordan named him Moose in honor of his favorite, Zeus the Moose.

Moose was a tiny dog, but his heart and his capacity for love were huge. Moose watched over Jordan with care and confidence. During Jordan's cancer treatments, Moose was always there to ease the pain and distract Jordan from the needles and tests. And when the treatments were so intense that they left Jordan feeling unusually sick, Moose never left Jordan's side. He'd kiss Jordan's face, as if trying to wipe the pain and tears away. The two of them were inseparable, and whenever Jordan was hurting or sad, his faithful friend was there to cheer him up and ease his pain.

The more time Jordan spent with Moose, the more content he became. Six months after getting Moose, Jordan died. But thanks to Moose, his final months were more bearable and comforting. Moose now lives with Jordan's parents and his two brothers. He is their last link with Jordan, and Moose's presence is a constant and reassuring reminder of the love Jordan helped foster.

———

Even just the image of an animal companion can help people—especially children—overcome the anxiety of being sick or hospitalized. It's as if children can become connected to an animal's image and turn that idea into a healing and safety mechanism. In one instance, a veterinarian realized the impact that even an animal story could have on children, and he transformed the AAT field with his version of "Josh."

An Image of Safety

The idea began when veterinarian Dr. Randy Lange's eight-year-old daughter Jessica was about to enter Children's Hospital in Knoxville, Tennessee, to have a tonsillectomy. Like most children, she was frightened of surgery and wanted some form of comfort. Dr. Lange began doing some research to find children's books that might help prepare Jessica for this "ordeal" (which he preferred to call an "adventure"). Unfortunately, Dr. Lange was not able to find anything for his daughter to read that he felt was current and helpful.

As a veterinarian, over the years he had observed the healing power of animals in the lives of children, so he had an idea. The culmination of this idea was a book titled *I'll Be Okay*, which Dr. Lange wrote once his daughter's surgery was complete. The story takes place through the eyes of Dr. Rick (named after Dr. Lange's deceased twin brother, who met an untimely death in a car crash) and Jessica's golden retriever, Josh. In the story, Josh actually goes through the experience of being checked into the hospital, and as he goes through various procedures, he is constantly reminded that he'll be okay. Josh also goes through the same emotions children have, from not being afraid to cry to the happiness of going home when he gets well. In addition to writing the book, Dr. Lange had a stuffed animal named Josh designed.

His idea has flourished, and today the Children's Miracle Network (CMN), which involves 170 hospitals coming together to support children going through hospitalization, has adopted the "Josh Project" as one of their major fund-raising efforts. Marie Osmond and John Schneider are both actively involved as celebrity founders and spokespeople for CMN. Josh has been adopted as the four-legged CMN Champion, and for participating hospitals, the book comes with a plush golden retriever stuffed dog. Whenever possible, Dr. Lange makes visits with the live Josh to some of the hospitals.

Since Dr. Lange first published the book in 1997, there have been many examples of the healing power Josh and his story have provided for children. One of the most profound stories came from Daniel, a father in Kansas City, Missouri. His daughter, Alicia, was being hospitalized for brain surgery. Here is her story of how the healing power of Josh had a positive impact on her life.

Powerful Medicine

In August 1997, seven-year-old Alicia began a difficult medical journey. Doctors diagnosed her with a tumor of the brainstem. She immediately underwent a 10-hour operation to remove the growth. But near the end of the procedure, life-threatening complications developed. The surgery was prematurely terminated, and after three hours of uncontrolled hemorrhaging, Alicia's blood miraculously clotted.

Although it saved her life, the blood clot subjected the delicate brainstem to pressure-induced trauma. As a result, Alicia lost total motor control of all voluntary muscles. For the next two months, she could not smile, frown, move, talk, eat, or walk.

Throughout 1998 and 1999, Alicia made slight but definite neurological improvements. But by the spring of that year, she began to regress, and after many tests, doctors found a fluid-filled, granulation tissue cyst on her brainstem. Surgery to remove the cyst was scheduled for Monday, August 30.

On August 20, Alicia was informed of the treatment plan. She adamantly opposed surgery and pleaded for its cancellation. She reminded everyone that the original surgery nearly killed her. She was scared and was completely content to endure her debilitating symptoms. Doctors recommended that Alicia consult the hospital's child psychologists.

Meanwhile, back at work, one of Daniel's coworkers was extremely concerned about Alicia. As a gift, he gave Daniel something that he thought would help. When Daniel opened the note, he read, "Meet Josh. Josh's story is intended to provide comfort to children who are facing surgery or a hospital stay. I hope Josh can help Alicia."

That night at bedtime, Daniel introduced Alicia to Josh and read her his story. Alicia readily identified with Josh's situation: doctors, blood work, examinations, radiographs, IV fluids, anesthesia, and surgery. As Daniel continued reading, he could see that Alicia was holding Josh tighter and tighter. Suddenly, Josh's credibility was innocently challenged: Josh's surgery was over, and Alicia asked if he had a scar from the incision. Daniel turned Josh over; Alicia closed her eyes (she didn't want to see it) and extended her finger. Daniel placed her fingertip on the midseam. She moved her finger over it, back and forth. She opened her eyes and visually inspected the "scar." Apparently satisfied, she gave Josh another hug. Josh had passed the test.

After that, Alicia no longer resisted surgery. She was still scared, but Josh convinced her that it's normal to be scared, that he and her family truly loved her, that he would be by her side throughout the surgery, and that she would be okay. Alicia's appointment with the child psychologist was no longer needed and was canceled.

On the day of the surgery, Josh accompanied her to the hospital. The nurses put a hospital ID band around his paw and decorated his ears with happy stickers. Alicia was clutching Josh as she was transported down to surgery, and Josh remained next to her in recovery, in ICU, and in her hospital room. In addition, Josh was correct—surgery proceeded uneventfully, and Alicia is okay.

Even though Alicia never met the "real" Josh, his spirit kindled hers and gave her the comfort and encouragement she needed in order to face and overcome a scary medical situation.

A Helping Hand

DURING A health crisis, the healing presence of a companion animal—be it a living, breathing ball of fur (or of feathers or scales) or a stuffed animal that comes alive—can set the stage for what some of us see as miracles. Companion animals have a loving, nonjudgmental, and empathetic nature that can bring out the best in people in even the most difficult situations.

Our companion animals not only help us with their behavior; they also offer us an important life lesson. When we become a loving presence in the lives of those we care about, we, too, can have a strong, positive effect on someone who is ill. Being by a friend's or loved one's side during an illness can help the healing process. Only when our internal spirit is kindled and nurtured can we have the will to overcome a health adversity. Regardless of any medical intervention, a person's internal desire very often plays the biggest role in healing, for our bodies cannot truly get well unless we feel loved and comforted and our minds are clear and focused.

Because of animals' ability to display unconditional love and friendship, they are often wonderful catalysts for the healing process. Their ability to comfort without saying a word is a skill we all need to master.

PET LESSON #5:
HEALING

Exercises: How to Use This Pet Lesson in Your Everyday Life

1. Try being a loving presence to someone who is sick. Too many times people are fearful of interacting with those who are ill. Some might be afraid of catching the illness, but most of us just aren't sure how to act in the sick person's presence. Educate yourself about a loved one's illness so that you can be a true source of support and encouragement.

2. Realize that illness is a trying time for people. While you may think that "just being there" isn't enough, it truly is. If a person who is ill tries to push you away or hurt you with their words, hang on to a positive and nonjudgmental attitude. Notice how the interaction changes when you keep a "healing" attitude.

3. Go to someone who could use your support, like Zeus did with the man in the wheelchair. Do you know anyone who needs help and could relate to

you or a situation you've been in? Be there for that person and be willing to open up about the challenges you have faced. Don't underestimate the power of your experience or your presence.

4. Think about the sick and elderly people you know. How can you help them connect with a companion animal? If you have a special companion animal who you believe can help others, look into animal assisted therapy and see if you and your animal can get involved.

5. When you are feeling out of sorts or ill, seek out an animal and feel their comforting presence. Let them feel your gratitude and appreciation.

6. The next time you feel your blood pressure rising or you feel anxious or fearful, picture yourself in the presence of a loving animal. If possible, be with one. You'll feel yourself calming down—we're never too old to have a "Josh" around.

7. Be loving, nonjudgmental, and empathetic with yourself. Picture a loving "you" helping and supporting the "you" who might be angry or disappointed with yourself.

8. Know that you can heal yourself through your attitude. Be kind to yourself—like Nugget was to Bill, like Sasha was to Joe, or like Zeus the Moose was to Jordan.

CHAPTER SIX

Lessons of Grief and Dying

Interregnum
The span between life and death
Can be as quick and sudden
As a puff of wind
That blows out a candle.
But the candle does not suffer
After darkness comes.
It is the person
Left in the dark room
Who gropes and stumbles.

—HELEN DUKE FIKE

NO MATTER WHERE we live around the world, we all share a common experience: grief. We all have to endure the pain that follows the death of a loved one. Whether it's a parent, sibling, friend, spouse, child, or pet that passes, grief grips us. For some it's all-consuming and debilitating. For others it is a reminder of their mortality. Feelings of shock, helplessness, abandonment, sadness, confusion, guilt, and anger can take what seemed like a normal, predictable life and turn it upside down in a matter of seconds.

Of all the human emotions, grief is often described as the most complex and difficult to handle. Grief is a normal reaction to loss. It is a deep distress that comes about in response to bereavement. Each one of us grieves in our own way and in our own time. There is no "normal" grieving process or period; it remains a unique and very individual experience. If not allowed to work through grief, we can stay stuck in a quagmire of our own emotions. Moving forward in our lives becomes impossible when we are lost in grief. Once on the other side of grief, many report an acceptance that allows them to go on.[1]

Unfortunately, our culture doesn't adequately prepare us for loss and death, whether we are grieving or trying to be helpful to someone who is grieving. We often feel awkward observing someone who is grieving. Consoling words are well meaning, but they don't erase the pain. Some of us encourage the mourner to move on, to overcome grief with the least amount of pain and discomfort. We often set a mental time limit for the mourner to grieve: a year, for example. If we are grieving, we can feel like we're a burden to those around us. And we often perceive the message from others, even when no one is sending it, that we should get on with our life. If we can't seem to do that, we begin to doubt ourselves and think there is something wrong with us—yet it is impossible to force the grieving process forward.[2]

The fact is that we cannot dismiss the very real emotions associated with grief and death and dying. We must go through them if we are to heal. So how can we get the support we need when we are grieving? Without saying a word, a companion animal can help us work through the many levels of grieving we experience, be it grief over the death of a loved one, a divorce, even the loss of a job. Having a pet's gentle love and companionship during a time of loss enables us to work through our emotions. I believe that part of an animal's ability to assist with grief lies in its nonjudgmental nature. While friends and family typically want to help us get over the loss, a companion animal helps us get through the emotions. Companion animals allow us to be ourselves as we grieve, in whatever form that takes, and offer accepting support as we deal with the phases of grief in our own time.

Although not recommended as a replacement for therapy and support groups, companion animals can help us get through grief. Their patience is limitless, and they have no agenda for our grieving. Their gift is their desire to stay with us during the hard times, snuggling close as we weep, scream, or pace the floor. Our pets appear to listen and to reach out to us in their own comforting ways. Experts suggest these are among the best ways anyone can support the bereaved.[3] Through our companion animals, we can learn that acceptance and resolution is within reach because whatever we do or say along the way is okay with them.

Stages of Grieving

IN 1969, Dr. Elisabeth Kübler-Ross proposed that there are five stages of death and dying: denial, anger, bargaining, depression, and acceptance. Although these stages have become the accepted blueprint for grieving, some argue that grief is two different processes: what we go through to prepare ourselves when we have advance notice for a loss and what we go through after the loss has occurred.

Founders of the Grief Recovery Institute, John W. James and Frank Cherry, challenge Ross's stages of grief. They propose that gaining awareness, accepting responsibility, identifying recovery communication, taking action, and moving beyond the loss are the stages that are critical to resolution of grief and loss.[4]

I believe there is a pattern to grieving that involves the stages of shock, denial, depression, anger, and acceptance. (Bargaining doesn't appear to take place when the person who is being mourned has already died.) Through each of these stages, a pet can support our healing. With their ability to simply be there for their human companions, animals help us get through the various stages in our own due time.

The Long Good-Bye

Judy and Jim had known each other since age one. They were both born in Mexico, and their families were always close. While growing up, even though they attended different schools, they went to the same parties and had the same social circle. As they entered their late teen years, it seemed obvious that they would expand their friendship and become romantically involved.

Throughout their dating years, their closeness strengthened. They could discuss absolutely anything with each other. They felt like soul mates. Their long and rich history made the decision to get married an easy one.

Those who knew Judy and Jim asserted that the couple had one of the happiest marriages in existence. When the union eventually produced three sons, the couple raised their children in the same loving environment that nourished their own relationship. As the children grew up, the family remained exceptionally close, and Judy and Jim were saddened when their eldest son left home. Deep down they knew the sadness they felt was just the beginning, as they still had two other sons who would eventually leave home to make their own way in the world. A few years after their youngest son left home, just as Judy and Jim were getting used to the empty nest, their oldest son, Patrick, returned to live with them to work with his dad in starting up an energy conservation company. But Patrick didn't come alone. He brought along his rottweiler, Maximalliano, or Max for short.

Jim and Judy loved to cook. They were both gourmet chefs by avocation, and they would often prepare meals in their large kitchen at the back of the house. That had always been the center of activity in their home. Shortly after Patrick and Max moved in, a pattern evolved. Nearly every evening, Jim, Judy, Patrick, and Max would enjoy dinner together and share their day. They'd talk about everything—current events, their jobs, Max's activities, and anything else that caught their attention. After dinner, Judy and Jim would take Max for a walk as Patrick cleaned the kitchen.

Neighbors joked that they could almost set their watches by those nightly walks. Each evening between 9:30 and 10:00, there were Jim, Judy, and Max walking the neighborhood. It was a great opportunity for Jim and Judy to have some time alone and to visit with people in the neighborhood.

As Christmas* 1997 approached, Judy began to find taking walks more difficult. She would often be out of breath after walking just one block. And the fatigue she felt was not ordinary tiredness. She remarked that it was an exhaustion she could feel right down into her bones. As the month progressed, she found it hard to even walk upstairs to the bedroom. Once she got upstairs, she would have to stop to catch her breath.

Judy was in exceptional physical shape and appeared much younger than her 57 years. Strangers often remarked that she didn't look a day over 45. So when the exhaustion grew worse, Judy knew she had to see a doctor. She made an appointment with her family physician, who diagnosed her with walking pneumonia and prescribed some antibiotics. Judy took her medication faithfully. When the medication had no effect, she revisited her physician. The doctor ordered a CT scan.

A day after the scan, Judy's doctor called her and said he found some "abnormalities" in her lungs. As the doctor was speaking, Judy felt numb. Her mind was racing, and with the medical terminology the doctor was using, she found it difficult to comprehend everything he said. All she distinctly remembered was the doctor telling her to come in for a biopsy. Judy saw the doctor the next day, still in a state of disbelief. The doctor tried his best to assure

Judy that they'd find out what was wrong, but she still wasn't hearing all his words correctly. Her mind was trying to protect itself from the emotional pain.

A week later, she received the results of the biopsy. Judy had a rare form of lung cancer. As the doctor said that dreaded "C" word, Judy went limp. Jim was beside himself. Neither could believe that someone who worked so hard to stay in good physical shape and who never smoked could have lung cancer. The doctor suggested an aggressive treatment plan that included chemotherapy.

Jim fought being devastated by the news. He knew he had to be strong for Judy. The woman he loved was about to begin the fight of her life, and he intended to support her in any way possible.

And there was Max. Throughout Judy's battle against cancer, Max proved to be one of her biggest supporters. As Judy lay in her bed at home, Max was often by her side. His big brown eyes seemed to say, "I'm always here for you." During Judy's chemo treatments, Max would often sit at her feet with his big brown head placed in her lap. Judy would stare into Max's eyes, petting his soft head and stroking his silky ears while the treatments invaded her body and attacked her cancerous growths. After the treatments, Judy often felt nauseous and weak, and Max would sit with her until she felt able to walk around again.

For the next 10 months, Judy and Jim did everything they and the doctors could think of. Despite their attempts, she was getting sicker and sicker. Her cancer was spreading, and she was having a hard time standing or even keeping food down. But even as the disease ravaged her body, her spirit remained strong. She was determined to fight her cancer until the very end.

On Christmas Eve, after having everyone over for dinner, Jim noticed that Judy's ankles were very swollen. He knew this was a bad sign, so he brought her to the hospital, where she received around-the-clock care. Her kidneys were failing because of the cancer growth, causing protein to leak into her blood system and produce edema. After some initial tests, the doctors told Jim and Judy that there was little they could do at this point. Judy, who wanted to die with dignity, asked the doctors to release her so she could die at home. The family arranged through a hospice to get Judy home and keep her as comfortable as possible during her final days.

Lying in her cozy bed off the kitchen where the family always congregated, Judy rested. The day was Saturday, and the weather was unusually warm for a winter day. Outside the sun shone brightly, and as the sunbeams cascaded through the window, they cast a warm glow on Judy's face. That afternoon, Patrick and his girlfriend, Charlene, came to Judy's bedside to give her some cheerful news. "Look, Mom, we're going to get married," announced Patrick. Then Judy's future daughter-in-law showed Judy her diamond. Judy looked at the ring, smiled, and said, "Whoopee!" As the word escaped her lips, so did her last breath. Judy died just as she wanted—at peace, happy, and surrounded by her family.

At that instant, Jim's world came crashing in. He had lost not only his wife but also his best friend and soul mate. Not at all sure about how he would get through this, Jim turned to his family for support. And although he dearly appreciated his sons' presence during the next few weeks, Jim found his greatest solace in Max.

During Judy's illness, Max had slept near Judy to comfort and protect her. Now that she was no longer there, Max began sleeping with Jim each evening. He'd sleep at the foot of the bed, never intruding more than Jim wanted. It was as if Max sensed that Jim simply needed his presence to feel comforted.

Jim continued the nightly walks with Max after Judy's death. As they walked, he would reminisce about all the good times he and his wife had over the years. He used the time to "talk" with Judy in his mind. It was his way of keeping her memory alive despite the all-consuming grief he felt.

When Patrick got married and moved out, he and Charlene were fearful that Jim would become lonely. They decided to leave Max with Jim, and they also bought him another dog, which Jim named Carlota, or Carly. Carly was a puppy, so she required a great deal of Jim's time and attention. Between housebreaking and obedience training, Jim hardly had a moment alone. "Max and Carly gave me the support I needed," says Jim. "Carly really needed my nurturance and guidance. As I attended to her, I began to let go of thinking only of the past. It's pretty hard to not be in the present when you have a puppy licking your face."

Jim credits the support of his family, friends, and particularly his two rottweilers, with helping him work through his grief. Although nothing will ever fill the place Judy had in Jim's life, he now looks forward to each new day, knowing that it is his to make the best of.

A Shoulder to Cry On

WE HAVE little control over certain life events, such as death, disability, and sickness. How we react to such situations often determines how we get through them. For those who are interested in human–animal interaction, the question of whether a companion animal helps in the grieving process is a valid one.

Dr. Karen Allen interviewed several widows who were dog owners to learn how their pets had helped during the profound life-changing event of losing their husbands. The descriptions they gave of their dog's role were nearly identical. The women said that they appreciated the kind words and support from friends and family but that what they really wanted was to be alone with their dog. This was partly because the dog had been a mutual companion for the women and their husbands, but more important, the dog insisted on no social pretenses to "buck up" and get on with life. With the animal, they could let their emotions show without anyone evaluating them and their coping skills.[5] Allen's research suggests that animals can provide a unique kind of social support that cannot be duplicated by humans.

Easing the Sadness

When Lynn was 21 years old, she received a job offer that required her to relocate to Tampa, Florida, which was about 50 miles away from her home. Despite the distance, she remained very close to her family after she moved, often driving home on weekends. She was particularly close to her youngest brother, John. They were best friends. The two were only four years apart in age, so they had many similarities and common friends. Throughout high school they were very supportive of each other, and they would often talk for hours after school about friends, romantic interests, school activities, and future plans.

One weekend when she got to her parents' home, John was ill. His breathing was hampered, and he was too fatigued to walk downstairs and greet her. That Saturday, as John's condition continued to worsen, the family took him to the emergency room. The doctors diagnosed him as having pneumonia. They admitted him to the hospital for observation and administered some powerful antibiotics. The next day all seemed to be going well, and John was beginning to look better. He sat up in his hospital bed to read the comics, and he joked with Lynn as she read the local paper. Lynn was reassured and decided to leave that Sunday to return to Tampa.

That evening, a virus began to spread through John's body. He went from appearing to get well to slipping into unconsciousness. John died that evening, 30 hours after his original diagnosis. Lynn had just arrived back in Tampa when she got the news. "Lynn, come home in the morning," her dad sobbed into the phone. "Johnny is dead." The words were like a knife stabbing her in the stomach. "It can't be, it can't be!" her mind cried. That night, Lynn lost her baby brother and her best friend.

Lynn could not contain her grief. When she got to her parents' house, she burst into tears and demanded to see her brother one last time. "I'm sorry, Baby, he's gone," her dad whispered. Within a few days of John's death, Lynn sank into a deep depression. She refused to get out of bed and would not eat. The shock of John's quick passing tore at her heart.

Slowly she resumed work, but she wasn't the same. She was always depressed and wanted to do nothing but work and sleep. Aside from her professional life, she began shutting herself away from the rest of the world. Within a few months, she lost more than 30 pounds. A woman with a normally larger frame, Lynn was down to a size 2.

Throughout Lynn's ordeal, her boyfriend at the time, Rick, stayed by her side and wanted desperately to help her. One day he found a stray Irish setter roaming near a main highway. The dog had no collar and was scared and alone. Her brown-and-white fur was matted from neglect, and her ribs were clearly visible because of severe malnutrition. Rick named the dog Brandy and brought her home to Lynn. He knew that Lynn once had an Irish setter, and he thought she might enjoy having a dog again.

The minute Lynn saw the disheveled-looking dog, her eyes warmed. Brandy responded in turn, giving out a series of quick barks and wagging her tail excitedly. Perhaps she sensed that Lynn was going to be her new caregiver.

Brandy was in such poor physical shape that Lynn had to focus on bringing the dog back to health. She forced herself to get dressed and go out to the store so she could buy some pet essentials. When she got home, she fed

Brandy, then bathed her and brushed out her fur. Each day she spent more time tending to Brandy's needs and less time in her depressive state. As she did so, the dog transformed from skinny, mangy, and weak to shiny and strong. Brandy looked almost show quality. Lynn also went through a transformation. As she nurtured and cared for Brandy, she started to rejoin the world and let go of her depression and anger over John's death.

Every day Lynn would take Brandy for walks along the bay. She found that getting out and walking with Brandy helped clear her mind and gave her time to think about the feelings she was experiencing. She enjoyed those moments when she could just be herself and have the calm presence of Brandy by her side.

After John's death he was cremated. The family kept the remains for several months. At Lynn's request, they scattered his ashes in the bay one bright and warm spring day. This proved therapeutic to Lynn—during her walks along the water with Brandy, she always felt closer to her brother. Through the exercise she was getting from their daily walks, Lynn grew more energetic, and she also began eating again. She says, "It took me almost a year to feel reasonably normal again. I was really angry with God. Brandy helped me work through my anger and depression by allowing me to express those emotions without remorse."

Brandy lived with Lynn for another 13 years. During that time, Brandy saw Lynn through several relationships and her ultimate marriage to Michael. After Lynn's wedding, she noticed that Brandy was getting feeble. Her legs would often give out on her as she walked, and she soon became very lethargic. She was no longer playing with her favorite toys, and food held little interest for her. Lynn took Brandy to the vet, but because of her advancing age, there was nothing the doctor could do. The doctor advised Lynn to take Brandy home and keep her comfortable.

The next morning Lynn got up early and went to hug Brandy good morning. As Lynn wrapped her arms around the dog, Brandy took a deep breath and died. Lynn was devastated. "At first it felt like my brother had died again," explains Lynn, "but then I began to see this picture of Brandy joining John, and a calmness came over me."

That day, Lynn realized it was time for her to share with others the peace and solace she got from Brandy. Brandy helped Lynn get over the grief of her brother's death. And through her own, she taught Lynn that grieving is part of the completion of life.

A Reason to Live

DURING A major life transition, people can sometimes feel like outcasts within their circles of friends and family. Whether it is because of a loved one's passing or a transition like a divorce, the loss of a job, or the end of a cycle of life, such as when the last child leaves home, feelings of grief are normal. When we're in emotional pain, we often believe that no one can possibly know how we feel. Companion animals can raise our spirits and help us get through the challenge of a major life transition.

An interview study of 81 women widowed one to three years explored variables related to adjustment following the loss of their spouses. When asked how they felt others treated them, some women made such comments as, "I feel they patronize me" and "I'm a society dropout." The women who had pets referred to their companion animals in a loving and positive way and reported less loneliness after being widowed than those without pets.[6] The bond between the women and their companion animals was a great emotional comfort.

Tower of Strength

Barbara truly understands the human–animal bond that takes place. When her husband, Bill, died of cancer a year and a half ago, Barbara wondered how she could go on living. Her husband had been everything to her—her support, her confidant, and her best friend. The two were adventurers in life together, constantly traveling and discovering new places. They especially loved Florida's west coast, and they explored the coastline thoroughly while on their pontoon, *My Turn*.

Throughout his illness, Bill had urged Barbara to remain her lively and free-spirited self after his passing. Barbara, who wanted her husband's last days to be as peaceful as possible, assured him that she would fulfill his request. But as his body grew weaker and weaker, Barbara felt her spirit dissipating. She began wondering about the direction her life would take after Bill's death.

By spring, Bill's cancer had spread throughout his body, and his doctors warned that there wasn't much time left. Barbara took a leave of absence from work and spent every moment with Bill. Because of Bill's cancer, his vocal abilities were limited, so he would often lie in bed and listen as Barbara talked. Early one bright April morning, Barbara spoke to Bill about the beautiful day and an upcoming weekend visit from friends. When Barbara turned to him for some sort of nonverbal response, she noticed that he was no longer breathing. Her lifelong companion was dead.

Despite the fact that Barbara had been preparing herself for Bill's death, his passing devastated her, forcing her into a spiral of depression. After the funeral, when friends and family left to resume their normal lives, Barbara sat alone and lamented over her loss. She refused to eat and quickly became a pale, thin image of her former self. Friends, family, and coworkers noticed the change in her, but Barbara couldn't return to her normal, happy self. The pain was just too great.

Barbara and her boss, Wayne, had worked together for many years. As an executive assistant, Barbara had always been responsive to Wayne's needs. For years she had been proactive in anticipating his hectic schedule and priorities. He now watched her struggle to do the simplest of tasks. For Wayne especially, the change in Barbara's motivation was dramatic.

Wayne tried everything he could think of to bring back the Barbara he once knew. He offered her more time off with pay, but she refused. He invited her to his house for weekend cookouts, but she insisted she wasn't hungry and needed to be alone. He even offered to fly her home so she could spend some time with her family. She thanked him profusely but declined his offer. Barbara was lost in her depression and couldn't find her way out.

Since Wayne and his wife loved dogs, they suggested that Barbara might want to consider getting a dog. They told Barbara that when she was ready, they wanted to give her a new puppy. Barbara thought this was a generous offer, but, as with the other offers, she put it off. She didn't think she could bear sharing the space that she and Bill had built together with another living creature.

But as time passed, Barbara became more receptive to the thought of having a companion animal. She began to wonder if it might be nice to have someone to greet her every evening when she came home, someone to talk to at night, and, most important, someone to love again. A few months after Wayne's offer, Barbara gave her approval. She didn't have to ask twice. Wayne promptly found a golden retriever puppy at a local animal shelter and urged Barbara to come and see him. With some trepidation, Barbara joined Wayne and his wife at the shelter to visit this golden puppy.

When she and the puppy met, the puppy nuzzled her. Barbara's heart filled with compassion, and she broke into tears. But her tears didn't faze the puppy—he seemed to need her and readily gave her kisses and licks all over her tear-streaked face. Barbara could see that the dog would give her strength, so she named him Sampson.

Sampson quickly became Barbara's best friend, staying by her for support, running to her for affection, and simply being patient during Barbara's grieving process. There were many nights when Barbara couldn't sleep, so she'd bring Sampson onto the bed and allow him to nuzzle with her. The feeling of another living being in the same room with her made her loneliness more bearable.

Sometimes Barbara would yell at Sampson if he did something that disrupted her schedule. She would always feel guilty for her outburst, as Sampson would run to her whining, as if to say, "I'm sorry." The unconditional love Sampson displayed to Barbara showed her that it is possible to love again, even after such an incredible loss. His patience with her occasional outbursts of anger and disillusionment allowed her to heal faster.

Thanks to Sampson, Barbara once again had a reason to live. Sampson needed her, and she needed Sampson. Barbara slowly began regaining the weight she lost, and she found her cloud of depression gradually lifting. While Sampson is in no way a substitute for Barbara's husband, his love, affection, and companionship helped fill a void in her life, making her feel whole again. Her boss even allows her to bring Sampson to work. "Now he has become the company mascot," Barbara proudly reports.

Endless Love

RESILIENCY IS one of the hallmarks of childhood. Children have an uncanny ability to bounce back after a setback and still see the world as a happy and limitless place. Sometimes, though, death can overshadow a child's resilience and cast the child into a deep grief similar to an adult's. It's comforting to know that an animal's love and support helps not only adults but also children heal their grief. Through my own story below, I learned this from experience.

Recapturing My Innocence

One sunny Saturday morning in June when I was five years old, I was playing at my friend Donna's house. We were dressing up our dolls in various outfits and playing in her dollhouse when a neighbor came by to get me. "Go home, Mary," he said to me. "Your father is sick and he needs you there."

In a panic, I ran out the back door of my friend's house and hopped over the fence that separated our yards. I got to our back porch in time to find my dad lying there unconscious.

I knelt down to wake him up, but he wouldn't move. I started to cry and pleaded with him to open his eyes.

"Come on, Daddy," I begged. "Please wake up. I'm here now."

In the midst of my turmoil, I didn't hear the ambulance sirens and was startled when two paramedics pushed me out of the way. When I looked up, neighbors were surrounding us. Some of them were talking in a hushed voice. "The poor girl," I heard one woman whisper.

I watched as the ambulance crew got out a stretcher and gently laid my dad on it. The events were overwhelming to my young mind, and everything seemed to be moving in slow motion. I thought my dad was sleeping as his body was pushed into the back of the ambulance. That was to be the last time I saw my dad alive. He died of a massive heart attack en route to the hospital.

Grief-stricken, my mom lived in almost a comatose state for a year following my father's death. They had been high school sweethearts—he was the only man she had ever loved. I was left to fend for myself emotionally for that first year after my dad's passing. I learned to handle it by pretending that he was still at work and that he would eventually come home. When I could no longer pretend, I became very sad. My mom began to see my sadness. She decided that a companion animal might cheer me up and take my mind off my father's death.

She approached me one day and asked what kind of pet I would like to have. I was always fond of cats, so I told her that's what I wanted. That afternoon she took me to the local animal shelter and told me to pick out any cat I wanted. As I looked at the various cats waiting to be adopted, a beautiful gray-and-white longhaired Maine coon caught my attention. As soon as I saw him, the name "Cookie" came to my mind. I was delighted when my mother agreed that I could take him home.

Cookie was a special cat who had the patience of an angel. From the time I was six years old until I was 13, I considered Cookie my best friend. We were virtually inseparable. To an awkward, tall, intense child, Cookie was the perfect balance. He and I would spend hours playing together. Cookie would sit under my mother's green velvet chair and hide behind the fringe that hung from the bottom of the chair to the floor. I'd stick my hand under the fringe, and he would gently bat at my fingers from his vantage point. His big soft paws felt so good against my hand. I would laugh and squeal with delight for hours on end.

No one ever made me laugh like that delightful furry friend. His antics and love supported me gently as I grew up without my dad. Years later, of course, I learned that many people experience unexpected tragedy, but at the time I was just young, scared, and unable to understand. And it was the constant and faithful love of this delightful companion that bolstered me.

From Discouragement to Hope

IT'S IMPORTANT to recognize that it isn't only death that triggers feelings of grief. Other life changes, such as divorce or the loss of a job, cause people to feel depressed, isolated, and alone. When a marriage ends or a steady job terminates, people must cope with the transition to living alone, finding meaningful employment, battling negative self-esteem, and more.

In many ways, the emotions people experience when going through life changes are similar to what they go through when a loved one dies. They may appear outwardly depressed, may avoid family and friends, may not want to get out of bed, or may stop eating. Since any significant loss can trigger feelings of grief, those who are going through these trying times need a source of comfort and encouragement. During these profound life transitions, a companion animal can be that source.

Marlene M. Rosenkoetter, Ph.D., R.N., believes that a companion animal can help the grieving person reconnect with the world faster because the animal offers a safe, neutral topic of conversation, one with which nearly everyone is comfortable. She also points out that sharing our feelings with an animal helps us cope more effectively with the emotional pain and distress a life-changing event causes.[7] How does this happen? Basically, the animal needs care, and the person responds positively to being needed. This kind of interaction brings structure to a life that is lacking routine.

Comfort in Times of Need

After 20 years of marriage, Rosemary's husband sat her down one day and told her he wanted a divorce. The news left Rosemary speechless. She knew that she and her husband were having what she thought of as minor problems, but she didn't think the occasional arguments or differences in opinion warranted a divorce. She wanted them to work through their difficulties, but her husband refused.

He insisted that the couple had grown too far apart, and he wanted his freedom to start a new life.

At about the same time, their daughter left for college, and Rosemary's father, with whom she had always been close, was diagnosed with cancer. Between her divorce, her daughter's departure, and her father's illness, Rosemary felt like all the people she held dear were leaving her in some way. Her entire world was collapsing, and she didn't know where to turn.

One afternoon, as she sat on her sofa crying, wondering what she was going to do with her life, Rosemary began to feel that the burdens she was facing were too much for her to handle. She prayed for strength and support, in whatever form it might take. Just then, her beloved black toy poodle, Nicky, came over and licked her face. She sat with Rosemary as Rosemary cried, never looking away from her and keeping her body close to Rosemary's. Rosemary sensed that Nicky understood her pain and that she wanted to be there for her. She took Nicky in her arms, hugged her, and let the tears flow.

That afternoon was the first of many during which Nicky would sit with Rosemary as she cried. As the days passed, Rosemary's crying bouts became fewer and fewer. Nicky instinctively adjusted her behavior to Rosemary's. When Rosemary had a good day, Nicky would back off a little, but she would still observe her distraught friend. On days when Rosemary felt weak and weepy, Nicky was right there beside her, nuzzling her.

Six months later, the divorce was final. With Nicky's support, Rosemary was determined to go on with her life. When Rosemary began dating again, Nicky was right there checking out each of her suitors. She would greet each man warmly as she circled him. Her inquisitive stare always seemed to say, "I'm watching you. Be nice to my friend."

Rosemary eventually met Jackson. They fell in love and made plans for marriage. A month before the wedding, when Nicky was 14 years old, she began acting unusual. She was no longer able to jump onto the couch to nuzzle with Rosemary, and she showed little interest in anything but sleeping. Her breathing also became labored; she was continually struggling to catch her breath. Concerned, Rosemary took Nicky to the vet. After giving Nicky a thorough exam, the doctor had devastating news: Nicky's heart was failing, and there was nothing he could do. Nicky would continue to deteriorate quickly and would be in more and more pain. Upon hearing the diagnosis, Rosemary immediately burst into tears.

As Rosemary held Nicky in her arms, Nicky continued to look at her. Her look seemed to imply that she wanted to comfort Rosemary and take away her grief. The vet suggested that euthanizing her might be the best thing so that she wouldn't suffer any longer.

Rosemary wasn't ready to let Nicky go, but she realized that keeping Nicky alive in her condition would be selfish. Rosemary looked up at the vet and said, "Okay." The vet left the room to prepare a syringe so that he could give Nicky the injection that would end her suffering. Alone together, Rosemary and Nicky stared into each other's eyes for seconds that seemed like hours.

Tears streaming down her swollen face, Rosemary thanked her devoted friend for helping her through such trying times. Nicky, who seemed to sense that Rosemary was ready to let go, kissed her lifelong friend, took one last labored breath, then died. The vet came back into the examining room to find Nicky lying limp in Rosemary's arms. Although Nicky is gone, her spirit still lives on in Rosemary, who strives to always be the comforting friend to others that Nicky was to her.

Grief After a Job Loss

LIKE DIVORCE, the loss of a job can trigger feelings of grief. When we no longer feel that we can accomplish our professional goals or contribute to the family income, we can begin to think of ourselves as failures. In addition, we often rely on what we do for a living to give us our identity in the world, and losing that part of us is like losing a trusted companion.

Me and My Shadow

Kathy is an industrious mother of three who always prided herself on being a "supermom." She not only ran the household and cooked meals for her husband and three children but also had a career that contributed to the family's prosperity. Her ability to balance schedules and survive on little sleep were the keys to her successfully handling such an active lifestyle. She and her husband, Stan, were able to save for their children's education and still have money to spare for simple pleasures like boating and buying sports equipment for the kids.

Kathy had worked her way up the ranks and been promoted to the top administration position of a nursing home. She had 16 direct reports and 143 indirect. She worked 10- and 12-hour days and had a 75-minute commute each morning and night. Despite the long hours, to Kathy, it all seemed worth it. She felt effective in her career—her numbers were profitable, the patients were getting good care, employees generally liked being there, and she made her bonuses. Her family understood her hectic schedule and supported her in her career. They knew her profession was a huge part of who she was, so they did all they could to cheer her on and share in her victories. By all accounts, life for Kathy was good.

The following year, the laws governing nursing homes changed, and Kathy's employer filed for Chapter 11 bankruptcy, resulting in a completely different environment at work. But Kathy was resilient. She managed successfully in the new environment, and, although she was concerned about the new trend in her industry, she knew she'd be okay. She focused her energies on helping her fellow team members adapt to the changes. She put in even more hours than before, confident that the effort would contribute to the longevity of her career.

Unfortunately, Kathy failed to anticipate the day her boss and the regional vice president told her she was no longer needed. Adding to her pain, they followed company protocol and had a security guard escort her to her car.

"You've done a fine job, Kathy," her boss said to her as she left. "But we need to downsize, and we can put a person who is licensed in your spot who will cover two facilities." His explanation did nothing to alleviate the pain she was feeling.

With tears filling her eyes and rolling down her cheeks, Kathy managed to drive herself home. Once home, she called Stan at work and told him the news. He immediately came to her defense and kept telling her how unfair it was. He was angry, and although he meant well, his reaction seemed to create more stress for Kathy. When the children came home from school, they wondered why their mom was home from work. Kathy explained the situation to them. The children tried to understand what their mom was going through and what her lost income would mean to the family, but they soon became absorbed in their own lives.

Alone and feeling like a failure, Kathy curled up in her bed and cried the rest of the day. She told herself that no one would ever hire such an incompetent worker as she, and she wondered how she would ever find meaningful employment again. While she sank into the depths of self-pity and pain, verbally beating herself up, her new puppy, a black miniature schnauzer named Shadow, came into the room and begged to be on the bed with her. Kathy reached down and picked the dog up. For the remainder of the afternoon and evening, Shadow stayed by Kathy's side, helping her as she went through the shock of devastatingly losing her livelihood.

Shadow soon became Kathy's sole source of support during the day when the house was empty. All Kathy wanted to do was stay in bed and mope. She didn't want to search the classifieds for a new job, she didn't want to call former colleagues to ask for their help in her job search, and she didn't want her neighbors to know she was out of work. Her pride had been deeply damaged by the blow, and she felt like she couldn't face anyone but a family member.

Lucky for Kathy, Shadow seemed to have other ideas. To get Kathy out of bed, Shadow would come into the room with his favorite toy, hold it in his mouth, and sit up on his back legs, as if begging Kathy to play with him. Unable to ignore the dog's antics, Kathy would give in and play a game of fetch or keep-away with Shadow. Once out of bed for this activity, she started progressing with other normal daily tasks, such as showering, doing laundry, cooking, and reading the newspaper. The more Shadow begged Kathy to play with him, the more Kathy was able to concentrate on the present moment and begin to release the feelings of disappointment and shame.

Kathy's yard was fenced, and the family often allowed Shadow to go into the backyard for exercise and play. Since Kathy was now home with the dog, she began taking Shadow on daily walks around the neighborhood. In doing so, she met neighbors she had never spoken to, and before she knew it, she was networking with these people to find a new job. As she opened up to those around her, she saw that her possibilities weren't as bleak as she once imagined them to be.

Once Kathy started back into a regular routine, she felt much better about herself; however, there were times when the grief returned. It was those times, when she was alone and sobbing, that Shadow came to her side and affectionately licked her tears away. She would hold Shadow's face and thank him for loving her at her lowest and for not expecting anything in return other than her love. It was those quiet moments, when they were at each other's side and looking eye to eye, that helped Kathy back from a dark corner. Shadow helped her realize that she had more to be thankful for than to be sad about.

"Shadow was my lifeline," says Kathy. "He was empathetic when none of the family was able to be there for me. My life was turned around through my job loss. I know Shadow supported me through the transition and that his love and loyalty helped me to heal."

Within six months of losing her job, Kathy secured another position with a nearby nursing home. She believes that without the love of her furry friend, she would not have had the strength to continue to pursue her professional endeavors.

The Healing Circle

Fortunately, you don't need to be a companion animal's primary caregiver to benefit from its ability to help heal feelings of grief. Just as companion animals are taken into hospitals and nursing homes to assist those in physical pain, they also visit patients suffering from the emotional pain associated with grief, and the impact they have can be profound.

Elisabeth regularly visits nursing homes with her cat, Circle, a gray-and-white tiger–Maine coon. She rescued Circle from an animal shelter after it had been brought in as a stray. For the past two years, Circle has been vital to the well-being of many nursing home residents. When asked how Circle helps the residents get through their feelings of grief, Elisabeth recalled the story of an elderly woman who everyone referred to as "Sarge."

Sarge was a 77-year-old woman who used to be a sergeant in the U.S. Army. One of the women who paved the way for future female military officers, Sarge was extremely tough, independent, and used to giving orders. She was known to bark even the simplest of requests. Instead of politely asking someone for a glass of water, she was known to command, "Water! Now!"

Sarge became a resident of the nursing home shortly after being confined to a wheelchair. She had fallen and broken her hip, leaving her unable to care for herself any longer. Her harsh manner put people off and kept them from forming relationships with her. Whenever another resident or staff member tried to talk with her, she'd instruct them to leave her alone in her usual authoritarian style. She often could be seen sitting alone in a room or simply staring out the window.

One day when Elisabeth was at the nursing home with Circle, she decided to try to approach Sarge. With Circle in her lap, Elisabeth sat next to Sarge in the common room where the residents watched television. Sarge glanced over at Elisabeth and Circle, then continued watching television.

"How is your day going?" Elisabeth asked Sarge.

Sarge said nothing. She didn't even look in Elisabeth's direction. Not discouraged easily, Elisabeth asked another question.

"Would you like to hold the cat?" Elisabeth asked. "His name is Circle."

Sarge looked at Elisabeth and said, "I don't like cats." She seemed to be trying to stare Elisabeth down. Her eyes pierced deep into Elisabeth's soul, challenging Elisabeth.

Elisabeth said nothing. She just looked back into Sarge's deep brown eyes. After a few moments of silence, Sarge reached out and put her hand on Circle.

"He's soft," Sarge said. "Just like my dog."

Elisabeth remained silent. She sensed there was something Sarge needed to verbalize, and she didn't want to interrupt her. At about that moment, Sarge began talking about her dog, Ralph. She would utter a few phrases, then pause, a few more phrases, then pause, trying to keep her composure. When Sarge was done speaking, Elisabeth pieced together her story.

One day about five years before while Sarge was at the grocery store, two men broke into her house through a back bedroom window. They rifled through her personal belongings and gave the whole place a once-over but couldn't find anything of value—at least to them. Sarge had no expensive jewelry, no high-tech electronic equipment, no rare antiques, and no prescription drugs in the medicine cabinet. The robbers, who were obviously upset that their efforts were wasted, decided to take their anger out on the only thing they thought could possibly be of value to the home owner: the cocker spaniel, Ralph.

When Sarge came home from grocery shopping that day, she immediately noticed that something was wrong. Ralph, who usually greeted her upon every return, was nowhere to be found. Sarge dashed from room to room, calling out Ralph's name. When she arrived at the back bedroom, she saw that the window had been busted out, then she saw her beloved Ralph lying in a pool of blood. The robbers had shot him.

Sarge didn't have a support system, so she never spoke of Ralph's death. She kept her grief hidden deep inside and never let it surface, never giving herself a chance to heal. Seeing and touching Circle, however, was the stimulus Sarge needed to verbalize her pain about losing her dog.

Elisabeth believes that companion animals like Circle help people talk through their grief. She observes that most people aren't encouraged to tell the story of their loss or to talk about their departed loved ones. But, she believes, that's just what we need—to talk about our grief experiences openly and often.

"Circle has a knack for getting people to open up and talk about their feelings," says Elisabeth. "What I'm learning about grief is that it's embarrassing to many people. But having a pet around helps them come to terms with their feelings and express the emotions they so desperately want to hide from others."

Today, Elisabeth still brings Circle to nursing homes in order to help the residents work through their emotional angst. She is also a supporter of hospitals and funeral homes that employ a bereavement facilitator to help people through their grief. In doing so, these organizations send the message that it's okay to grieve and that "getting over it" isn't the ultimate objective.

Grieving the Loss of a Companion Animal

THE DEATH of a companion animal often triggers feelings of grief that can be as profound and long-lasting as when a human dies. Unfortunately, because our society tends to be unsympathetic toward pet loss, many people are embarrassed at the depth of their grief or believe that others will think of them as strange.[8] However, studies of people who have lost a companion animal have shown that more than three-quarters of the people interviewed experienced some type of disruption in their daily routine after the loss of a pet. In addition, more than a third said they took time off work after their pet's death, and another third experienced difficulties in their relationships with others.[9] Clearly, a companion animal's death can have a big impact on our emotional well-being.

After losing a pet, some people take another animal into their life immediately. Others wait many months or even years before they can bear the thought of another animal being in their life. Either way, it's a personal decision that must be given much thought.

An Unforeseen Bond

Dee always thought she knew how she'd handle the loss of one of her dogs. She asserted that she'd have to wait a long time before bringing another animal into her life, believing that adding a pet would prove too painful. Fortunately, fate had other plans for her.

During the summer of 1991, Dee and her husband, Dave, learned that their miniature schnauzer, Gretchen, had Cushing's disease, a condition that causes the body to produce too much of certain hormones, particularly corticosteroids or cortisol. Gretchen suffered from an enlarged abdomen, muscle weakness, lethargy, thinning hair, and a host of other symptoms. Just weeks after Gretchen's diagnosis, she died. Dee and Dave were heartbroken. Fortunately, they still had their beloved poodle-terrier mix, Heidi, to comfort them.

Heidi was a Christmas gift for Dave the same year that the Super Bowl broadcast was abruptly ended by the start of the movie that was her namesake. She came to Dee and Dave as a shiny black ball of fur with blue eyes, a cherry drop for a tongue, and the most loving personality imaginable. Her cheery bark warmed the heart of everyone who visited them.

Dee and Dave worked different hours (Dee had a day job, and Dave's schedule with the weather bureau fluctuated), so Heidi was often called upon to do some championship sleeping. She was always willing to spring up on the bed and snooze with whoever occupied it at the time.

Heidi must have had a way to store all that sacktime because on the weekends they'd take her to Brown County State Park, where she'd run the hills like an athlete. She'd then curl up in Dee's lap for the car ride home. Her gentle snoring always made Dee feel loved and needed. When Dee and Dave moved to Louisville, Kentucky, from Indiana, Heidi and Dave regularly played "chase the ball up the wall" in their basement. If Dave got tired of the game and Heidi didn't, that was okay—she'd drop the ball from the top of the basement steps and run down to catch it over and over again.

Six months after Gretchen's death, the unthinkable happened. Heidi, who was then an incredible 21 years old, fell into the backyard pool and drowned. Dee and Dave blamed themselves for Heidi's death, thinking that if they had only watched her more closely, she would still be alive.

At this point, Dee was virtually inconsolable. She loved both Gretchen and Heidi with all her heart and didn't know how she'd be able to live without her two precious dogs by her side. For the next few weeks she had a difficult time sleeping, and she rarely wanted to eat. She had the unshakable desire to shut herself off from the rest of the world so she could mourn her incredible loss. Dave's reaction wasn't much better. Although he hid his feelings better than Dee, he missed the two dogs dearly and felt as if a big spark in his life was gone.

Dee thought putting in extra hours at the office would help her work through her grief. She felt that if she kept her mind continually focused on something, she could better cope with her loss. One day, when she was going into work early, she decided to cut through a little town called Windermere, where the streets were dirt and the traffic clipped along at 25 or 30 miles an hour. She thought the leisurely drive would help clear her mind so she could focus on the day's tasks. What she didn't bargain for was coming upon an obviously car-challenged dog frantically wandering in the middle of the street. Cars veered to avoid hitting it, but none stopped to help. Amazed that no one cared for this little dog, Dee decided to rescue it and find its owner. But the dog had other ideas.

Just as Dee got out of her car to help, the dog raced down another dirt road. Dee followed in her car. The dog led her to the steps of a church. Dee sat down beside the dog and thoroughly studied it. It was a pitiful-looking black dachshund, very thin—its ribs were clearly visible, even beneath its long, scraggly, flea-infested coat. She asked it if it wanted to go with her. The dog barked at her. Its big brown eyes were filled with confusion and fear. Dee felt compassion for the animal welling up insider her, and she smiled at it. And as soon as Dee opened the car door, the dog jumped in.

When Dee brought the dog home and showed it to Dave, he was not happy. The dog didn't look the least bit appealing, plus Dave felt it was too soon after the loss of Gretchen and Heidi. He missed them too much to be able to give to another dog. But he was a gracious host and brought out dog food for their skinny guest. They were still unsure of its gender, but their intent was to simply feed the dog while finding its owner.

The dog was wearing a collar with a tag. The tag said "Murphy" and had a telephone number. They called the number, left a message, and patiently waited for a call back. Days later, when no return phone call had come, Dave called the humane society. He learned that Murphy had been there not once but at least twice. By now, however, Murphy had become "Samantha" and was forming a bond with Dee and Dave.

Samantha desperately needed attention, and Dee and Dave were happy to comply. At first the dog would jump on the couch and cuddle with them. Then she started staying on the couch for the evening. After a few weeks, she wanted to sleep in the bed with Dee and Dave. The couple obliged, both feeling that they needed the companionship of a dog after the loss of their two.

As the weeks passed, Samantha became a new focus of love and attention. On the days when Dee thought back to her beloved Gretchen and Heidi and felt sad, Samantha would be there to nuzzle with her and lick her tears away. Every Sunday, Dee would devote a few hours to grooming Samantha. With something to nurture and care for, Dee felt a sense of calmness that allowed her to open her heart once again.

Whenever Dee and Dave look at Samantha, they see an "angel dog," one who came into their lives totally unasked for and on a secret mission to heal their hearts. Samantha's love helped Dee and Dave through a difficult period and showed them that feelings of grief can subside in due time. Although they will never forget Gretchen and Heidi, Dee and Dave feel they have learned to accept their deaths better through Samantha's love. They know this "angel" has taught them a lot about healing a grieving heart.

⌒

Comfort in the Midst of Loss

GRIEF IS a very real and often debilitating emotion. Those with a good support network in place generally have a better time working through their grief and resuming a normal life. Companion animals are an integral part of that support system, for it is our animal friends that allow us to experience our own unique pattern of grief and its aftermath without forcing us to "get well fast." Their patient presence—no pushing, no prodding—sees us through the eye of the storm to a place of healing.

It's interesting how these life lessons are intimately intertwined. Grief involves losing someone or something we love, so without love in our lives, grief wouldn't be possible. Perhaps that's what makes grief so complex. It forces us to look deep within our souls to determine what truly is essential to us. When we grieve, we also acknowledge the importance of certain people and things to us as we restructure our lives to carry on without the lost person, animal, physical ability, or job. Grief also teaches us the importance of treasuring what we love and taking time to appreciate the important people and things in our lives.

By allowing our companion animals to be with us as we grieve, we open ourselves up to a new kind of love and support that is selfless. And after we experience the assistance an animal gives during the grieving process, we learn how simply having another living creature by our side can lessen our emotional burden. It's a lesson we can then pass on to others as they need consolation during their inevitable time of grief. It's a lesson that everything dies before it's reborn.

PET LESSON #6:

LESSONS OF GRIEF AND DYING

Exercises: How to Use This Pet Lesson in Your Everyday Life

1. What are you grieving about? Is there a loss that you haven't fully dealt with that keeps you stuck in the past? Make a list of your losses and determine which ones you have not yet accepted.

2. Who is part of your support system? How can you acknowledge their importance in your life? Is there an animal that can support you, like Barbara's dog Sampson?

3. Healing is a slow process. Set aside time each day to think of your loved one and snuggle up with a companion animal when possible. This is especially important if your pet is the last link with the deceased person.

4. If you experience the loss of a loved one, engage in a ritual like Lynn did. She would walk along the bay where her brother's ashes were scattered. What ritual can you use to keep memories alive while gaining closure?

5. If you are mourning the end of a relationship, like Rosemary was, or the loss of a job, like Kathy was, consider a companion animal to nurture you and to keep you focused on things other than your loss. What can you learn from this experience of living

with a companion animal that makes you a better friend to others?

6. The loss of a companion animal can make us feel sad and alone. Think about the ways you can honor your beloved pet and create a special ceremony to commemorate their contribution to your life.

CHAPTER SEVEN

Lessons of Playing, Living in the Present, and Staying Focused

"Present-moment living, getting in touch with your 'now,' is at the heart of effective living. When you think about it, there really is no other moment you can live. Now is all there is, and the future is just another present moment to live when it arrives. One thing is certain, you cannot live it until it does appear."

—WAYNE DYER

MANY OF US have seen two Labrador puppies wrestling in the grass, a young kitten pouncing on a rubber mouse, even dolphins playing swimming games. The fact is, all mammals play. And birds and other vertebrates exhibit social play behavior as well.[1] Whether it is wolves or dogs, wild cats or domestic cats, bears, bison, or horses, animals benefit from play in a variety of ways, including learning new social behaviors and having fun.

Just like animals, humans benefit from play. When we are young, we play intensely for hours with our peers. Playing house, outer space, soldiers, dolls, transformers, and doctor are among the many games that we might enjoy. While we're engaged in play, our concentration is focused, and we stay alert to what is unfolding in the game we've created. We're having fun, learning how to focus and live in the present, learning how to get along with others, role-playing adulthood, and more.

As we get older, however, most of us play less, which is unfortunate because having fun through play keeps us in the present. When play is absent from our lives, we can end up living more in the past and the future. I believe that regular play can help us be more effective in all that we do because it teaches us to stay "mindful," or "in the present," which is to maintain an awareness of the situation we're experiencing at that moment. It's hard to worry about the past or to obsess about the future when we are laughing with delight or challenged by a surprise in a game we're playing.

If we grow bored with what we're doing, whether it's playing a game or writing a business proposal, we check out mentally. That is often when we begin multitasking, which is practically the antithesis of living in the present.

In most developed cultures today, multitasking has become the norm. We spend time with our children, balance our checkbooks, and participate in a conference call for work—simultaneously. Multitasking has become the hallmark of a good manager in the workplace and certainly is reinforced. However, as multitasking becomes a life habit for many, we can wind up robbing ourselves of the present. As we talk on our cell phones while grocery shopping or answer our e-mail while eating a sandwich, our lack of concentration on any one thing can result in stress. We wind up feeling splintered, then wonder why.

Play is a way for us to take time to have fun and to concentrate on one thing. And perhaps most important, playing feels good and can make us laugh. Simply observing others at play, particularly children and animals, can be stimulating—and participating with them, a joy. When humans play or watch others playing, we are usually in a mindful state. Our attention is focused on what's going on and we're open to improvising in the moment. We can learn from play how to be mindful most of the time. Being mindful means we see the newness in even such routine events as going to the grocery store, pumping gas, and driving to work. When we give these regular activities our full focus, like when we play intently, we can glean new insights.

Staying in the Present

BESIDES BRINGING us pleasure when they play, animals can help us stay in a mindful state and improve our own ability to stay in the present by their example. When we are engulfed in worry or fear, play can be the kind of relief that sets us free of our own internal obstacles. Practicing mindfulness can also open us up to new information and perspectives.[2] Playing can help us be our best and most creative, both personally and professionally.

A New Focus on Play

Lori felt like her whole world had crashed in on her. Within weeks of being laid off from her dream job in women's sports, she and her romantic interest broke off a six-month-long relationship. To add to her emotional turmoil, her grandfather died on Thanksgiving Day. All these incidents happened within five months of each other, leaving Lori feeling overwhelmed. She often found herself ruminating about how things could have been different. As the days passed, Lori had a hard time not worrying about her future, and she finally decided she had to move back home for a while to live with her parents. Throughout it all, the only constant in her life was the bond with her "boys," Pounce and Lewis.

Pounce is a 16-pound orange tabby with a proud and seemingly stoic nature. He loves to lie on Lori's chest and knead her arms and shoulders with his furry paws. Lewis is a white shorthair with black markings and a huge appetite.

He weighs in at 23 pounds and loves to cuddle up with Lori as much as possible. Lewis is outgoing and becomes fast friends with those who meet him. He likes to follow Lori around the house.

The loss of her job, her love interest, and her grandfather kept Lori down. After she moved to her parents' house, she didn't want to do anything. But there was one thing that was able to get her out of her doldrums—watching the antics of her loving feline companions. Lori's work schedule had often been hectic, and she had never had the opportunity to be at home with her pets during the day. But now she was around—and she marveled at the play adventures the boys engaged in each day.

Lori discovered that Lewis and Pounce routinely play a game that involves chasing each other around the house. She calls it "run and seek." Each cat takes a turn running around the house while the other hides under furniture. The hidden cat then blasts out of his hiding place in order to catch the running cat off guard. The greater the element of surprise, the longer the cats played. Watching this helped Lori forget about her current situation and enjoy the moment she was in. "Their antics keep me focused on now," Lori remarks. "It's hard to stay in the past or worry about the future when you see how much enjoyment the cats get from the present. It's contagious."

Lori no longer had the hustle and bustle of getting ready for work in the morning, so she didn't have to dash from the shower to the car. And that freed her to learn the intricacies of her cats' daily "bathtub games." When Lori is finishing her shower, Pounce and Lewis get excited. "Sometimes Lewis butts his head against the door as if he is saying, 'Are you done yet?'" Lori observes. One of their favorite games is to sit in the tub after it has emptied and roll in the remaining drops of water. Then they play "attack the shower curtain" by jumping up against it and hitting their feet in a bicycling motion against the plastic liner. As they slow down the pace, the boys will sit in the tub and, almost thoughtfully, watch drops of water fall from the faucet. "I soon found myself joining in with their play." Lori says. "It feels great to just be with them and laugh."

While Lori was searching for another job, she'd turn to the newspaper's classified section for possible employment leads. The sound of the newspaper crinkling was all Pounce and Lewis needed to create another game. As Lori would read the newspaper, Pounce and Lewis would go underneath the scattered paper and pop their heads out from under the print. Their cute antics would interrupt Lori's internal dialogue, which was often nothing more than self-recriminations, like: "What's wrong with me?" "Did I go to school for the right thing?" "Why is this happening to me?"

Lori believes that the love and playfulness of her cats inspired her to go on with her life. She started running again—something her former busy schedule didn't allow time for—and began to play golf. As she played more, she also stayed in the present, stayed mindful of her current situation, and "things just started to fall into place."

Lori now has a fulfilling job and her own condo. She has just begun dating someone who she feels is special, and she has plans to go back to school. But with all the new activities, she still isn't forgetting the lesson she learned from the boys. Every time she finds herself not staying present in a situation, she thinks about playing with the cats. And when she can, she actually joins in with their game.

What Play Can Teach Us

DURING CHILDHOOD, play is an integral part of life. Play is the natural mode of learning, and by interacting with others through play, children learn the rules and regulations of adult life.[3] As adults, we often don't get a chance to play with others. We become so wrapped up in the complexities of adult life—the business meetings, the family commitments, the yard work, the car pools, and the deadlines—that we forget the importance of losing ourselves in a fun and challenging game.

Lessons from an Angel

Like most people, Allen and Linda Anderson live busy lives. Between their careers and personal commitments, they sometimes feel as if they don't have a moment to spare. They both travel frequently for business, and in addition to their jobs, they work on numerous animal projects. They are the authors of *Angel Animals: Exploring Our Spiritual Relationship with Animals.* They are also the cofounders of the Angel Animals Foundation, a nonprofit charitable organization that "increases love and respect for all life, one story at a time."

The Andersons are the proud "parents" of five companion animals, and they try to arrange their schedules so the animals are never alone or with a sitter. While the animals enjoy this arrangement, it often means that either Allen or Linda is home alone with the animals while the other person is away. Having time for just the two of them is a rare occurrence, so when it does happen, they cherish the moments.

One bright June day, Linda returned to their home in Minnesota after consulting with a client in California for five days. Allen picked her up from the airport. For the first time in many months, the two of them were going to have a few days to spend together. As they walked out of the airport terminal, they marveled at what a rare occurrence this was for them. They talked eagerly of all the things they could do together to have some fun. They were as giddy as two schoolchildren suffering from a case of puppy love.

But as the drive continued, their conversation began to drift to business talk. They discussed Linda's most recent work assignment, the upcoming trip Allen was going on, the deadlines for the Angel Animal projects, and the housework and home repairs that needed to get done. By the time they arrived home, they felt overwhelmed by all the tasks they needed to attend to. Although they were looking forward to their time together, their workload realization put their personal plans on hold. They both secretly dreaded all the work that would keep them apart during their time together.

When they opened the door, their animal family greeted them enthusiastically. The warmest welcome came from Taylor, their yellow Labrador retriever. She wagged her tail furiously and slobbered both Linda and Allen with kisses. Allen and Linda greeted Taylor in return and kissed all the other animals "hello" before retreating to their home offices to tackle their piles of work. But before Linda could put her bags down in the foyer, Taylor ran into Allen's office and brought out her favorite yellow tennis ball. Looking at Taylor, knowing what the dog wanted, Linda said to Allen, "Why not? It's such a beautiful day. Let's take a break before starting our work and have some fun. We can go for a walk by the lake and have some ice cream." Allen wholeheartedly agreed.

As the three of them drove to the lake, Taylor was a bundle of excitement in the backseat. She paced from window to window in anticipation of their final destination, and she squealed with delight the entire ride. Allen and Linda were so amused with Taylor's antics that they focused solely on her and forgot to talk about all the impending tasks.

When they arrived at the lake and Allen opened the back door, Taylor bounded out of the car and was jumping with excitement. Linda got out of the car and observed how the late afternoon sun, still surprisingly high in the sky from June's long days, cast a warm glow on the shimmering water. She immediately felt at ease and relaxed. Allen went directly to the ice cream stand and bought three frozen treats—two in cups and one in a cone for Taylor. As Taylor ate her ice cream, she slathered the frozen dessert all over her face. Allen and Linda broke into laughter at the sight of Taylor's face covered with vanilla ice cream.

They couldn't have asked for a better evening. The gentle breeze cooled the sun's rays, and the soft, cool grass under their feet felt like plush carpeting. They went to the lake's edge, and Allen hurled the tennis ball into the water. Taylor immediately ran after it. She carefully made her way over the rocks and jumped into the lake in search of her toy. She grabbed the ball in her mouth and made her way back to Allen. Allen took the ball from her mouth and threw it again.

By the fifth throw of the ball, the process was becoming almost mechanical to Allen. So as he engaged Taylor in this game, he and Linda began conversing about work again. They began making to-do lists for later that evening and the next day, and they started prioritizing the tasks that needed to get done first. Their fun and relaxing outing was quickly diminishing. Before long, work was their only focus again, and they decided it was time to head home.

Allen stopped throwing the ball and told Taylor to go to the car. But Taylor was not done playing; she had something in mind. She walked over to Allen, knocked the ball from his hand, ran with it in her mouth to the shoreline, swung her head, and threw the ball into the water. Before jumping in to retrieve it, she turned and looked at Linda and Allen as if to say, "You're being too serious. We need to play some more." When she came back with the ball, she dropped it at Allen's feet. She looked up at him with her big brown eyes and seemed to be pleading, "Let's have some more fun before going home. Come on. It's your turn."

As Allen and Linda looked at their dog, all they could do was laugh. It suddenly dawned on them that Taylor was right—they had forgotten how to play. But through Taylor, they were learning how to play and about how important play is. With Taylor's encouragement, they admitted that the work would still be there the next day and that they needed to enjoy their time at the lake together in order to recharge and refresh their minds. Allen and Linda always knew Taylor was a special dog, and that day she taught them how to play so they could lead more balanced and focused lives.

A Mindful Approach to Play

JOY AND HAPPINESS are often associated with play and can help people and animals with "becoming at one with the activity."[4] Studies of the brain's chemistry during play indicate that various neurochemicals that cause feelings of elation in animals are emitted at different times in the play cycle.[5] Therefore, play is not only fun but is also good for us. By becoming fully engaged with any activity, we can experience the event on a whole new level. The more we take in the events around us and concentrate on the here and now, the more mindful we become.

How often do we drive somewhere, only to realize that we don't remember driving the route at all? It's as if we're on autopilot. Think of everything we miss seeing and experiencing as a result of our oblivion—the trees, the other cars, the scenery, the pedestrians, and so on. But by increasing play time, we can learn to be more mindful in all kinds of situations—and see what we've been missing during those drives.

Mindfulness is an Eastern principle that deals with a heightened awareness of how we interact with our environment and what's going on in it. It is often associated with meditation in that regular meditation teaches us to concentrate in a mindful way. In his book, *Skillful Means,* Tarthang Tulku describes mindfulness as "a combination of concentration, clarity, and awareness brought to bear on even the smallest details of experience."[6] It is about staying fully present to whatever is going on in the moment.

The concept of mindfulness can be seen in various aspects of life. One of the secrets to Phil Jackson's success as a basketball coach is his use of mindfulness with his players. In his book, *Sacred Hoops,* Jackson describes how he trained the Chicago Bulls to stay mindful on the court so that each play is a new response to the last one.[7] When they're mindful, players don't think about the past shot or what the score might be at the end of the quarter; rather, they learn how to stay relaxed and how to play the game in the present moment.

The same concept holds true in our daily lives. Too often we are stuck in the past or preoccupied with the future. Instead of focusing on what's present in our lives and enjoying the moment, either we dwell on what we should have done last week, last month, or last year, or we waste our energy second-guessing our future moves. While reflection and planning are important, we cannot get so caught up with them that we lose sight of the gift of today.

In her book, *Mindfulness,* Ellen Langer defines the key qualities of a mindful state as an openness to new information, an awareness of more than one perspective, and the willingness to create new ways of thinking or doing something.[8] Langer also proposes that adults often become "mindless" as we perform many tasks again and again. This mindlessness can lead to our no longer enjoying the present and to reduced creativity. In animal play research, some scientists are reporting a link between play and creativity. The thinking is that play can help animals increase their competence, and with greater competence, they are more likely to use novel behavior in situations they have mastered. Play can also be effective in training animals to handle unexpected challenges in social and physical environments by increasing the flexibility of their behavior.[9,10] It is the use of new or novel behaviors that spawns creative thinking.

Current research on animal play shows some exciting possibilities. Animals play to learn, to prepare for unexpected situations, and to reduce their emotional stress in new situations. In other words, play enhances the ability of animals to emotionally cope with the unexpected, thereby increasing their chances for survival.[11] Through the unexpected situations that occur in playing, animals learn to regulate their stress with their play partner and with the environment so that when a new or dangerous situation comes up in life, their emotional state is easier to control.[12] Such was the case with Howard and Burt.

An Animal's Contribution to Our Mindfulness

When Howard's secretary innocently asked him, "Do you like cats?" he had no idea that he was about to meet one of the best friends he would ever have.

"Sure, I like cats," Howard responded. "In fact, I've had a few cats over the years." With that, his secretary began telling him about an abused five-year-old Siamese cat she had rescued but could not keep because of her husband's severe allergies. Having a pet hadn't crossed Howard's mind in years, and he was not sure he wanted one. However, he agreed to stop by his secretary's home after work and at least meet the cat before making any decisions.

The moment Howard saw the cat, he knew he would take him home. While the cat had a Siamese look, it was stockier and less "pointy-nosed" than what Howard envisioned as Siamese. The cat had a perfectly symmetrical dark mask, white breast, and dark legs with matching white "boots" on all four paws. As his secretary carried him close, Howard could see a combination of gentleness and fear in the cat's eyes. He could not imagine how someone could have mistreated this beautiful animal. He took the cat home that night and began a 12-year-long relationship with his new friend Burt.

When Howard and Burt got home that evening, Howard opened the cat carrier, and Burt darted out and scurried under the sofa. Howard tried to coax him out with some food, but Burt was too scared to comply. Realizing that it would take time for Burt to adapt to new surroundings and to trust Howard, Howard put the food dish on the floor and left the room so Burt could eat in peace.

In the days and weeks that followed, Howard treated Burt with consistent kindness. Burt gradually became comfortable, then affectionate, with Howard. For some months, he still hid if anyone else came into the house. But eventually he learned that there was no danger and began to greet company with curiosity.

As Burt overcame his shyness, he began displaying his mischievous side, sometimes to Howard's annoyance. For instance, when Burt wanted a snack, he would climb up on the refrigerator, open the cabinet doors, knock the cereal boxes out onto the floor, and open them, scattering cereal in every direction. Howard quickly learned that raising his voice in anger brought Burt back to his past timid behavior. When the cat cowered in fear of being struck in response to a raised voice, Howard felt terrible. After the first incident, Howard was careful to use a stern tone but not a raised voice as he communicated displeasure to Burt.

Over time, the two grew increasingly close. Burt would sleep in the crook of Howard's arm most nights. If Howard was not in the position Burt wanted when Burt got onto the bed, Burt would sit on Howard's chest and patiently stare until Howard moved his arm to make room.

Burt was very playful, and Howard found that playing with Burt had an impact on his work that he would never have predicted. Howard was partner in a marine construction company. His day was typically consumed with operational issues, so taking work home in the evenings was the only chance he had to work on more strategic issues and other matters that required blocks of quiet time and creativity. But this presented two challenges. After a long, draining day, it was difficult to feel alert and creative in the evening. And if he worked until bedtime, he found his mind often continued to dwell on work, making it difficult to get to sleep.

But Howard found a solution. He discovered that playing with Burt before starting his paperwork cleared his mind and refreshed and relaxed him in a way that made him much more productive and creative. Similarly, playing with Burt after he finished working for the evening cleared his mind again and relaxed him before going to sleep.

Over time, Howard and Burt developed a repertoire of games and some tricks that Burt would do to entertain visitors. Burt's favorite game was "under the sheet." Howard kept an old sheet in the living room. He would throw the sheet over Burt, then tap at it with a small plastic wand. Burt would wildly chase and swipe at the wand from under the sheet. Then Howard would roll Burt up in the sheet and they would wrestle, with the sheet providing some protection from Burt's claws. Burt even learned to drag the sheet out to signal that he wanted to play.

As Burt's trust grew, so did his tolerance for being handled in various ways. Howard would announce to company that Burt could do somersaults and could country-western dance. The somersaults consisted of Howard picking Burt up under his front shoulders, supporting Burt's back with his forearms, and flipping Burt over to land on all fours. To dance, Howard would lift up Burt's front paws so Burt stood on his back legs. Then, to country music, Howard would gently pull Burt forward to the slow-slow-quick-quick cadence of the Texas two-step. Burt seemed to enjoy the laughter and applause like a born performer. And the more games Burt mastered, the more confident he became around strangers.

Burt died at the ripe old age of 17, playful almost to the end. The 12-year-long relationship with Burt left a profound mark on Howard's personal and professional life. Thanks to Burt, Howard learned the critical role that consistent kindness plays in building trust and how enjoyable that trust could be. He has used a similar approach in dealing with people over the years and feels that the result is an unusually broad circle of wonderful, close friends. Playing with Burt before and after his evening work also taught Howard that even briefly putting aside thoughts of past and future and enjoying the now can have an enormous impact on clarity of mind and creativity.

Play activity doesn't have to be so hands-on to evoke a mindful state. Sometimes simply watching animals in their natural environment can trigger mindfulness in humans. Take the story of a writer named Paula who learned how to focus better and be creative during a dry spell.

Mindful Observation

Paula is a poet. She sees the beauty in everyday things and captures the imagery in words. By the end of an unusually long winter, she was having difficulty writing. She was anxiously awaiting the arrival of spring. The fickle March weather was teasing her by providing springlike temperatures one day and harsh temperatures of winter the next. She desperately needed to shake her wintertime blues in order to get some inspiration for her poetry. She longed for a way to refocus her mind and energy so she could create magic with her words.

One evening her husband brought home a new fish for their aquarium. Two of the three blue discus fish and one black ghost fish had died during the winter, and Paula and her husband had decided their tank needed new life to celebrate the arrival of spring. Paula also hoped a new fish would inspire her poetry.

Her husband arrived with a clear bag containing water and a rare albino oscar fish. Paula got excited when she saw the fish. "Wow!" she exclaimed as her husband put the new arrival in the tank. She couldn't take her eyes off it. Watching it made her feel peaceful and happy. They named the fish The Healing Light.

The next day, Paula sat on her living room sofa trying to write, but nothing was coming to her. She stared at her blank page, her mind racing with a thousand unrelated ideas that she couldn't join into one coherent thought. Just then, she looked up at the fish tank and observed The Healing Light. The large oscar fish, approximately 10 inches from nose to tail, floated gracefully in the tank. To Paula, it resembled a ballerina. The fish's faint peach color around its bottom reminded her of a tutu. As her eyes progressed up the fish, she was almost mesmerized by its almost translucent fins and white upper half.

The longer she watched the fish, the more her mind calmed. Soon she was able to focus her thoughts again. As she concentrated on the fish, she put her pen to paper and began writing poetry. That day she wrote three new poems.

Paula affectionately refers to The Healing Light as her "spring fish," as it brought a spiritual revelation to her in the springtime. "Watching The Healing Light taught me that sometimes the smallest things can mean so much," says Paula. "Whenever my mind is racing or the day gets too stressful, I simply watch my oscar fish and feel at peace immediately. Every day, he teaches me to slow down and to enjoy the present moment." Paula feels fortunate to have such a simple gift that can touch her soul and rekindle her spirit.

Staying focused and in the present involves letting go of past hurts and old ways of doing things. It doesn't mean that we don't learn from our past experiences; rather, it means that we are willing to suspend our mental models to consider new approaches.

Present-Day Lessons

For as long as he can remember, John has always had cats in his life. Their free-spirited nature and loving disposition made them ideal companions for him, as he, too, strove to live with an unconventional zeal and independence. He loved watching cats play and enjoyed the quiet presence of feline companionship after a hard day.

A few years after John's most recent cat of 14 years passed away, he was ready to get another. So John visited the local humane society and asked if they had any gray, declawed tabby kittens—just like his previous cat. He quickly learned that the humane society doesn't approve of declawing cats, and he feared that he may have blown his chance of getting a cat through them. The lady at the humane society told him, "If we get one in, we'll call you." To his surprise, three months later, the humane society called John informing him there was a declawed cat available for adoption.

Upon arriving at the humane society, John discovered that the cat was black and full grown. He still wanted a gray tabby kitten. He also learned that the cat had been found trapped in a storm drain. She was very sick, malnourished, and dehydrated when she came to the shelter, and the people at the humane society had nursed her back to health.

As he sat in the meeting room with the cat, she walked two or three steps, then stopped to scratch. John deduced that she had fleas. He just didn't think she would be a fit for him. However, he decided to give the meeting some time and at least act like he was remaining receptive.

When the cat finally came over to John, she meowed and rubbed on his right shoe. John melted. He decided to adopt the cat and called his vet from the humane society. The doctor told him to bring the cat by on his way home. The doctor examined the cat, gave her some shots, and, much to John's relief, issued her a clean bill of health.

When John brought the cat into his San Francisco apartment, he was sure she was going to spend hours checking out her new turf. He was wrong. The cat sniffed around for five minutes, then slept for three days—getting up only to eat and use the litter box. This alarmed John, but once she got the rest she needed, she turned into the most affectionate cat he had ever had.

As was his style, John didn't give the cat a conventional or usual name. Instead, he chose not to call the cat by any name. Sometimes, however, he and his friends would call her The Goddess, or John would call her Little Mother. As the years progressed, he realized that Little Mother was appropriate, as the cat was always teaching John something new.

The most profound lesson came early in their relationship. Once Little Mother felt comfortable in her new home, she began letting her mischievous side show. She would chew on plants and knock them over onto the floor, spilling potting soil everywhere. She would also open drawers and scatter the contents all over the house. John would always reprimand Little Mother, and when he did, the cat would lay low for three to five minutes. The next moment, Little Mother would be back in the present. She didn't hold on to those negative feelings like humans so often do.

This doesn't mean that Little Mother didn't learn from her actions. If she did something that hurt her, like jump up on the stove while it was hot, she learned never to do that again. If she did something that John wasn't pleased with, like chew the ivy, she learned to stop that, too. Little Mother doesn't forget the past, nor does she hold on to it.

As John says, "Little Mother is in a zone that is about 10 minutes on either side of the present."

By observing Little Mother and being open to her teachings, John has learned more about staying in the present. Instead of letting past events control him, he stays focused on what is occurring now. John works diligently at not being concerned about events that have already transpired or about holding on to past experiences with others. While he acknowledges the happenings of the past and doesn't ignore them, he believes that focusing on the present is the only way to turn a bad situation into a good one and a good situation into an even better one. With Little Mother's guidance, John is reminded that it's always better to let go of the past and stay in the present.

Games for the Soul

FOR ADULTS to embrace play and present-moment thinking, we must stop regarding play as idle time. As our world has become faster, more mobile, and more technologically advanced, we have adopted the notion that being busy means we're productive. However, unless we engage our minds and bodies in playful activities and learn to focus our thoughts on the here and now, we become only more scattered, more stressed, and sometimes less competent at our tasks. Play offers the mental break we need to recharge and revitalize our mind, body, and spirit. It allows us the opportunity "to be" versus "to be always doing."

When we're focused and rested, we perform at our best. So instead of thinking that there's no time for play in our days, it's time we learn from our animal companions that play is beneficial and that we should play often. Just as food nourishes our bodies, play nourishes our spirit. By engaging in play and truly focusing on the activity at hand, we can gain the mental clarity that leads to greater happiness and a stronger connection to the world around us.

PET LESSON #7:

PLAYING, LIVING IN THE PRESENT, AND STAYING FOCUSED

Exercises: How to Use This Pet Lesson in Your Everyday Life

1. Think back to the last time you had fun playing a game with another person or animal. What were you doing? What did you learn?

2. Take time to play with a pet. Is there a dog you can play ball or another game with, like the Andersons did with Taylor? A cat you can engage like Burt?

3. Watch others play. What do you notice about what's going on? How do you feel? What's the impact of play on them? On you?

4. How mindful are you most of the time? What are some of the ways you can give your full concentration and focus to everyday tasks and projects you're working on?

5. How often do you multitask throughout the day? Are you really accomplishing more by doing two things at once, or are you doing two tasks less competently? The next time you begin to multitask, stop and think how much more effective you might be if you focused on one task or event at a time.

6. As Lori watched Pounce and Lewis play, she began to let go of her past disappointments and became more resourceful. When you're feeling concerned about the past and nervous about the future, find some animals or children and watch them play. Now allow yourself the opportunity to play with your options and have fun exploring possible next steps in your life. What can you do here and now to enjoy and learn from this experience?

7. Play every day for a week and see how you feel at the end of the week. If you record your observations in a journal every time you play, you may gain even greater insights.

CHAPTER EIGHT

Lessons of Being a Humble Hero

"Everyone is necessarily the hero of his own life story."

JOHN BARTH

HOW DO YOU define a hero? Who do you think of when you hear the word "hero"? Do images of Mother Teresa, Martin Luther King Jr., or Neil Armstrong flash in your mind? Or do you envision fantasy characters such as Hercules, Superman, or Wonder Woman? In reality, heroes are ordinary people, much like you and me, who find themselves faced with an emergency and respond to the need. From the person who rushes into a burning building to save a child to those selfless individuals who aid in disaster relief efforts across the country, these everyday heroes often remark that they were just doing what they thought was the right thing.

Sometimes these heroic people, motivated by love, courage, or even guilt, sacrifice their own comfort to do good deeds for others. Why do they do this? It can't be for material gain. Maybe for the satisfaction of making the world a better place? Or because it would be too painful for them to live with the knowledge that they turned away when their efforts were needed most? Whatever the reason, many of us depend on these everyday heroes not only to save lives but also to serve as role models of bravery.

Similarly, many of our animal companions risk their lives or endure pain and discomfort to help others. Like many of their human counterparts, they ask for nothing in return. They are humble heroes who go out of their way to help those in need. I am inspired when I hear stories about the companion animal's ability to sense a problem situation and act boldly and assertively.

In recent years, our animal heroes have received more attention. In various countries around the world, annual awards are given to animals who have made a difference. For example, the Los Angeles SPCA regularly issues a request for nominations for its annual "Hero Dog Award." It is described as "the award that symbolizes the heroic acts performed by dogs to save and protect people." Any California dog is eligible for this award, and it is advertised as "the highest honor bestowed on a companion animal." Past winners include a police dog hit by a bullet intended for its partner, a poodle that alerted a sleeping family to a fire, and a rottweiler that brought a portable telephone to its owner, who called 911 while having a heart attack.

There's no doubt we benefit from heroism every day. Many people have been saved by acts of selflessness and have, in turn, helped others when circumstances demanded it. Whether we think we have heroic tendencies or not, we can let animals remind us of the importance of being heroes in our own lives.

What does it mean to be a hero in your own life? Being a hero in your own life is about living the values that you hold dear, such as integrity, respect, and service to others. It's also about challenging yourself to grow and learn despite the inconvenience. Our inner heroic journey is about transforming our own level of consciousness, whether we risk overtly through obvious physical sacrifice or covertly as we fight our internal demons to be in alignment with the values we want to live. How do you become a hero in your own life? I believe that each one of us has the opportunity to be the hero in our own life—if only we don't miss the chance. We can look to many sources for inspiration. Heroism is a common theme that continues to draw and engage us all. From the *Odyssey* in Greek mythology to the adventures of Luke Skywalker in *Star Wars,* we are attracted to and can be inspired by the stories of heroes past, present, and future. As humble heroes, our companion animals can also inspire us. They are reminders of the journey that we can all take. By saving a life, our animal heroes model the courage and responsiveness that are essential if we are to live in a more caring world together. They teach us to continue to be heroes in our own lives.

The Basics of Heroism

WHEN ASKED, many people equate heroism with physical strength and courage. The image of a great, fearless warrior who rushes in and saves the day predominates. If that's the case, then what constitutes heroic behavior? Is it being fearless and risking your life to save another, or is it persevering in some task, whether physically dangerous or not, in spite of fear?

As far back as Socrates, people have been questioning the virtue of courage—what it is and how they can attain it. By studying wartime soldiers, researchers have found some common characteristics of those who display "courage": self-confidence, having the skill to do the required task, high motivation, a sense of responsibility, and the desire to avoid disapproval.[1]

In recent years, much research has been done on psychiatric patients who have overcome debilitating fears, such as agoraphobia and the fear of germs. Researchers have found that the patients approached what scared them the most to help them get beyond their psychological obstacle—definitely courageous behavior. Yet these people who persevered and acted courageously are not usually considered heroes. Why not? Perhaps this is proof that we cannot relate heroism to strength or courage alone. Rather, we should expand the definition to include those acts that strengthen our character and contribute to the greater good.

When we acknowledge as heroes those whose actions benefit other living creatures, our deserving companion animals join the ranks of heroes. By not limiting our perception of heroism to physical strength or acts of courage, we can see the true heroic acts that occur every day, such as animals alerting people to danger, sniffing out diseases, or following their instincts to protect someone from immediate harm.

The stories we routinely hear about animal heroism are truly amazing. In Buenos Aires, a dog saves a four-year-old boy from a swarm of bees by covering him with his body; in Wyoming, a rottweiler pulls a drowning three-year-old girl out of a canal; in California, a dog pins a five-year-old girl to the wall during an earthquake, getting her out of the path of a falling microwave oven; in Iowa, a dog saves a 32-year-old man from three would-be robbers. The list could fill volumes. Remarkably, none of the animals in these situations had been trained to act in a certain way. They were simply "doing the right thing" when the need arose.

Heroic animal stories are typically about dogs—for good reason. With their superior sense of smell, dogs can detect scents that humans can't, and the larger breeds are strong enough to pull humans to safety. Cats can be heroic, too—consider the true story of Muffin, a calico cat that saved her human family from danger.

Alertness to Danger

One cold December night, a large and stunning calico cat showed up on Dan and Daniele's doorstep. At first Daniele figured it would wander away, but its incessant meowing indicated otherwise. An animal lover all her life, Daniele was not about to turn her back on the cat and force it out into the cold Maine night. She fed it and found it a spot to sleep, and the next morning she began looking for its owner. She could tell by the cat's well-kept physical appearance that it had been someone's house pet. Adding fuel to the search was Daniele's husband, Dan, who wasn't pleased with the new arrival, as the family already had three dogs and a cat. Daniele ran ads and put up posters locally to find her new feline friend's lost family. Despite her efforts, no one came forth to claim the cat she now began to call Muffin. The family soon grew very fond of Muffin.

One month after Muffin's arrival, the family cat, Norman, appeared very ill. He grew more and more lethargic and no longer wanted to eat, so the family took him to the vet. After some tests were run, the doctors determined that Norman was suffering from kidney failure. Within a few days of the diagnosis, Norman died. The children (twin preschoolers—a boy and a girl—and an older son) were heartbroken. The twins had grown up with Norman. He had lovingly put up with being chased around the house and having his ears and tail occasionally pulled. As they grieved for their lost playmate, Muffin set about comforting the children. She nuzzled with them whenever they cried and even began imitating the antics Norman used to do to make them laugh. Muffin then went on to repay her new family even more for their kindness.

On January 12, 1999, the twins were in preschool, and Daniele had planned to pick them up and do some errands. But she had an unexplainable feeling that she should go directly home after picking up the twins. She tried to ignore it but couldn't.

When Daniele and the twins got home, she began to make their lunch. For some reason, Muffin was acting up. She was meowing loudly and in a distressed way. Daniele kept telling the cat to "wait a minute," but Muffin wouldn't stop. Finally, Muffin went upstairs and began making noise by pushing her body against the master bedroom door, and then when there was no response, forcefully throwing herself against the door. When Daniele went upstairs to settle Muffin down, she instinctively opened the door to the master bedroom. To her horror, she saw flames shooting from the closet. In a panic, she grabbed a blanket from the bed and attempted to put the fire out. The blanket caught fire. Daniele then went to get the cordless phone to call the fire department, but she couldn't find it.

Part of the house was engulfed in flames by the time Daniele found the phone in the living room and called 911. She grabbed the twins and ran to safety at a neighbor's house. When the firefighters arrived, Daniele realized that Muffin was still in the house. One of the firefighters went back inside and found Muffin huddled in the closet of the twins' room. He grabbed Muffin and made his way out of the thick smoke and hot flames.

That day, Muffin was a hero. Daniele added, "What's worse is that I have my hairdressing salon in the basement. I was planning to put the kids down for a nap after lunch and then go work in the basement. I would have never known about the fire without Muffin's insistence—she saved our lives!"

Because of her actions, Muffin won the International Cat Association's Trophy for Heroism in 2000. Even more rewarding to Daniele is that her husband, Dan, who had never really connected with animals in the past, has finally taken to Muffin. He now pets her and talks to her lovingly on a regular basis. Apparently, Muffin has shown him how committed and heroic cats can be.

Heroic Instincts

PART OF an animal's heroic ability lies in its instinctive nature. For years we've heard stories of animals being trained to rescue stranded people, search for drugs and weapons, detect land mines, and even alert and protect people with physically unnoticeable medical conditions. The question always was, "How do they do it?"

According to some researchers, it's all a matter of an animal's sense of smell. Throughout the ages, as people's brains have grown, we've lost the need for our sense of smell, depending instead on our brains to analyze, reflect, and get us out of precarious situations. Animals, on the other hand, still rely on their basic instincts. In fact, a dog's nose is so sensitive that it can detect fingerprints on a piece of glass six weeks after a person has touched it.[2] When it comes to those dogs who can alert people to upcoming seizures, scientists tell us that what the animals are smelling is a chemical in people's bodies. And when the body is stressed, chemical changes occur that tell the animal something is wrong. The animal then reacts as trained.

A Heart for Heroism

Dakota is a heroic dog who uses his instincts to protect his human companion. Abandoned as a young puppy, Dakota was suffering from heartworms. The Golden Retriever Rescue Club of Houston nursed Dakota back to health and searched for a suitable human companion for him. They made a perfect match.

After suffering two heart attacks and undergoing open-heart surgery in January 1992, Mike was left with major heart damage and unstable angina. His health problems were further complicated by pulmonary disease, major depression, and stress-related anxiety. Because of his physical deterioration, Mike had given up on life and had planned to end it. He simply could not accept that his life as he knew it had ended. He had always been an active person who enjoyed both his work and his family. Now he couldn't even visit his parents or friends for fear that he might have an angina attack while driving. In his mind, his illness had taken everything from him, and this was the focus of all his attention.

Mike needed a reason to live. In 1994, Mike's doctors recognized that he needed help. They knew he needed something to get him excited about life again. They suggested a therapy dog. They believed a dog would be the push Mike needed to get up and out of the house, would make him move and exercise, and would demand attention and not let Mike forget that he was needed. That's when Mike met Dakota.

In the early part of their relationship, Dakota would beg Mike to play with him and take him for walks. Mike regarded this behavior as "a big pain in the neck." He wasn't used to something always demanding his attention. Although he was unhappy with his current life's circumstances, he was unhappier to have to share it with another living being. As it turned out, however, Mike soon became grateful for the attention Dakota showered on him.

The first time Mike had an angina attack in Dakota's presence, the dog laid next to him and pushed on his chest to help relieve the pain. Mike wasn't prepared for what Dakota was doing, but he wasn't in any condition to push the dog away. Instead, Mike encircled Dakota with his arms and held him. During that time, he imitated Dakota's breathing rate to keep himself from hyperventilating when the pain was intense. Once the pain subsided, Dakota remained, cuddling with Mike for two hours in order to keep him warm. Dakota's training hadn't included these actions, yet this same scenario played out during subsequent attacks. Mike soon began developing a bond with Dakota and wanted them to be together at all times.

Over the next year and a half, Dakota developed the additional ability to sense when Mike was about to have an angina attack, and he started alerting Mike to the oncoming attacks so he could take his medication before the attacks began. Today, Mike knows that when Dakota pulls on his arm, an angina attack is on its way.

Thanks to Dakota's presence, Mike's depression eventually lifted. He can now sleep at night, knowing that if he is about to have an attack, Dakota will alert him. Mike can also go for walks now and can freely socialize with his friends and family again. As a result, Mike is now back at work full time, with Dakota by his side each day.

"Dakota taught me how to love again and how to see life with new eyes," says Mike. "He made me have meaning and purpose again. Dakota and I routinely go fishing, to the store, and we have a life together that's getting better every day."

Even more remarkable is that Dakota's ability doesn't work only around Mike. Dakota recently alerted one of Mike's colleagues of an impending heart attack. Wisely, the man took Dakota's warning seriously and went to a hospital emergency room. Within minutes of stepping into the emergency room, the man suffered a heart attack due to a major blockage. Being at the hospital for prompt attention most likely saved his life. A heart attack usually builds up over 8 to 10 hours, so Dakota was able to pick up the smell and alert the man in plenty of time.

As a result of Dakota's heroic service, he was awarded the 1999 Beyond Limits Award from the Delta Society, an organization that promotes and documents the science of healing the link between humans and animals. The society's Beyond Limits Awards recognize companion animals that enrich the lives of the people they touch. Dakota is definitely a worthy recipient.

Of Service to Others

TRUE HUMBLE heroes give themselves completely to the service of others. They are selfless, making sure the other person survives, and in many cases, shines. Nothing exemplifies this kind of giving more than the thousands of service dogs who assist people with disabilities and other medical ailments. Service animals can indeed be considered humble heroes, as they not only provide physical assistance and often help guide people away from danger, but they also offer companionship and foster a sense of trust, which aid in the person's emotional well-being.

Throughout time, humans have kept animals as a form of protection. To this day, many people regard having an animal, particularly a dog, as a reassuring contributor to their safety. Recent studies have even shown that people of all ages use animals to feel safe and create a sense of intimacy.[3]

While most people hear stories about a heroic action a service animal performed, very few of us are aware of the process animals go through to become classified as a "service animal." The next two stories cover both ends. One story is about the process that enables these animals to become "heroes;" the other is about how such heroic behavior can impact a person's life.

Heroic Training

John is the director of manufacturing for a book publisher. In addition to keeping up with his fast-paced publishing position, he raises and trains service animals. John socializes puppies that will eventually enter a guide-dog training program. He reports that it is a bittersweet experience because he must give away a puppy that has lived with him for 18 months. The entire process is truly amazing. Just like a companion dog raised in a home, a guide dog in training becomes part of the family. Trainers take them everywhere—to dinner, to the grocery store, to work, to visit a neighbor, and so on. The only time the dog goes outside is with the trainer or to relieve itself. As trust and love build between the family and dog, it becomes harder to let go. But for John, the vision of the dog helping a person in need mitigates the pain of saying good-bye.

Several years ago, the Marin County Guide Dog School gave John a beautiful male German shepherd named Flex. Flex was seven weeks old when John got him, and John raised him for 18 months. John had the responsibility of teaching the young, high-energy puppy such things as patience and discipline, and he was often at wit's end trying to calm the dog or get him to listen. John says that in training Flex, or any of the puppies, the most rewarding part is the patience he learns.

Through it all, John and Flex developed a sense of trust toward each other. "Trust is the essence of working with any guide dog," says John. "Flex and I developed a very strong bond. It was difficult to bring him back to the guide-dog school for further training."

As a result of John's efforts and other volunteers working with young guide dogs in their homes, disabled people around the country receive the assistance they need.

The Hero's Eyes

Pat went blind in 1991. Prior to that, she headed customer service worldwide for a major computer company. Because of a congenital condition that had been hastened by the high stress of her career, her eyesight slowly deteriorated, eventually resulting in total blindness. A year after losing her eyesight, Pat attended Southeastern Guide Dogs, Inc., based in Palmetto, Florida, where she got her guide dog, a black Lab named Bart. Knowing herself, her type A personality, Pat asked for a strong dog that would respond quickly and adeptly. "I thought that I could treat Bart like a rental car," she said.

Because Pat was very control oriented, she had difficulty taking orders from others. Therefore, allowing Bart to guide her and instruct her where to go was a difficult release of control for her. There would be times when Bart would slow down and Pat would overstep him. She'd walk into trees because she'd override his guidance. Pat still wanted to be in control and stubbornly ignored his lead. Her trainers worked with her until she finally "learned her dog."

Pat was bound and determined not to let her new disability slow her down. In her first year with Bart, they accumulated 100,000 air miles. But all those miles wouldn't have been possible if Pat hadn't learned a very important lesson during her and Bart's first business trip together. That's when Bart showed Pat that she could trust him to do his job.

Pat and Bart were staying at a New Orleans hotel for a business convention. About 5:30 A.M., Pat took Bart out behind the parking garage to relieve himself. The bell captain offered to go with her, but Pat snapped at him, saying, "I have to learn how to do this myself." As they walked toward the grounds behind the hotel, Bart started to disobey Pat's commands.

Despite Pat's attempts to get the dog to walk around the building and do his business, Bart began leading her in another direction. Pat resisted, but Bart was strong, and his determination didn't falter. Then she felt his fur brush up against her leg, and she could tell it was standing on end, so she reluctantly followed him. It felt like they were making a big U-turn, and Bart's route led them to the front of the hotel. When they got to the lobby, Pat couldn't contain herself. She began yelling at Bart, "You stupid dog. I'm taking you back to the school."

Just then a woman who was on her way to her housekeeping job at the hotel came running toward them. She said, "Madame, please don't yell at your dog. I was looking out of the window of the bus, and I saw the whole thing. A man stepped out from behind the stairwell. He had a gun, and he was coming at you. I told the bus driver to stop when I saw that you were walking right toward the gunman, but he wouldn't. Your dog was getting you out of danger and made you walk in the opposite direction."

After the lady explained what had happened, Pat fell to her knees and began to hug Bart. The action he had taken is called "intelligent disobedience." At that moment, she was overcome with love for him. She says it was like a spiritual experience—a warm wave of emotion swept over her, and she hasn't been the same since. The experience made her realize that Bart knew what he was doing and that she had to relinquish control.

That day Pat and Bart became a true team. Pat learned that she needed to be dependent on others, and she also learned she could trust Bart. Now she takes time for her friends and family—something she neglected in the past. Her confidence has also risen, and she now concentrates on the important things in life, like "taking a two-mile walk and enjoying each morning." But the most important lesson Pat says she learned was that it is possible to "turn an adversity into an adventure."

Today, Pat no longer works for the computer company. Instead, she writes and travels the country to speak at schools, civic clubs, and other organizations about overcoming adversity and guide dogs. "Bart is a special dog because he helped me to be the real me," says Pat. "Animals bring us executive types in touch with reality. All they want are the basics, like food, water, and affection. I was so busy chasing the almighty dollar, but Bart's heroic act showed me what life is all about."

⌒

Scientific research has begun to validate the role service animals play in people's lives. In 1995, a two-year study by Dr. Karen Allen et al. found that people with disabilities who had service dogs had better psychological well-being and higher self-esteem than those without service animals. People with disabilities who are dog owners also integrated into the community better and were able to exert more control over their environment. Other studies cite the findings of improved independence and social acceptance.[4] Obviously, service dogs are of great benefit to those who need them. And the sense of protection and security are on top of the many tasks service animals are trained to do.

Beyond Their Service to Humans

WHILE THE heroic acts animals perform for their human companions are remarkable, what's even more remarkable are the animals' heroic acts for other animals. When we hear stories of a cat rescuing a dog or vice versa, it makes us realize that true heroism knows no boundaries.

Nine Lives

Back in the late 1960s, Jan had a Saint Bernard named Mysteria of Manhattan (Misty for short) and a beagle named Max. One day, Jan's mother was out running errands, and she drove by a woman who looked like she was doubled over in the street, possibly having a heart attack. When she pulled the car over to help, she realized that the woman didn't need help. She was doubled over because she was stuffing puppies down the sewer. She said that her dog had mated with the wrong dog and that she didn't want the "mutts." The woman had already thrown down all but one, and Jan's mother grabbed that one.

She immediately took the dog to the vet, and when he checked out all right, the family decided to keep him. They named him Bandit because of the cute little brown mask across his black face.

A few days after Bandit joined the family, Jan, her mother, brothers, grandmother, and neighbors had all gathered in the front yard, talking and enjoying themselves. The dogs were in the backyard by the pool. All of a sudden there was a tremendous amount of barking, but nobody thought much of it.

Then Misty started to howl painfully, and her barks got louder, so some of them decided to see what was going on. When they got to the backyard, they saw that Bandit had fallen in the pool and Misty had gone in and pulled him out. She was standing by the pool with Bandit's neck in her jowls.

Luckily, Jan's grandmother knew CPR and pumped the water out of Bandit. Within minutes, he was fine. Misty was a heroine. Thanks to her, Bandit lived for 13 years. And Bandit showed the family and Misty such strong love throughout those years that Jan is convinced he knew he had been saved, not once but twice.

Sometimes these heroic acts between animals are based purely on instinct. What we see as a truly amazing feat is simply an animal performing a basic act that it has used for centuries to survive. In today's world, we sometimes get so caught up in using technology to give us the answers that we ignore our internal instincts—those "gut" feelings that tell us what to do. If we learn nothing else from the heroic acts of these animals, let it be that we should follow our instincts and do what we "feel" is the right thing. In following our instincts, we'll be helping our own growth and also a fellow being—human or animal—in need.

Maternal Heroism

Cathy witnessed these heroic animal instincts firsthand through Kannah, her mixed-breed dog. In addition to Kannah, Cathy also had a male cat named Copper. One day Copper brought home a girlfriend, and it was quickly apparent that the female cat was in heat. No matter how often Cathy tried to separate them, they'd find each other and proceed to mate. Weeks later, the female cat nestled under her front porch and gave birth to a litter of six kittens. Although Cathy wasn't happy with the situation, she decided to let the female cat stay on her property so she could nurse her kittens.

Shortly after giving birth, the female cat appeared to be in heat again, and she and Copper performed the mating ritual at every opportunity—even in the middle of the street. Sadly, one of their street escapades caused their untimely demise, as a car hit them in the midst of their passion. This left Cathy with six newborn kittens and no mother cat to care for them.

Cathy immediately went to the vet for advice. He gave her some kitten replacement milk and some basic instructions for caring for the newborns. Everything seemed to be going well until two of the kittens began having difficulty eliminating. At the vet's suggestion, Cathy tried stimulating the kittens' bottoms with a damp washcloth in order to mimic what a mother cat would do with her tongue. Despite all her attempts, nothing helped. Cathy was convinced the two kittens would die if they didn't eliminate soon. That's when Kannah stepped in.

Instinctively, Kannah took over all the duties of mother cat. She licked their bottoms, nuzzled with them, carried them gingerly in her mouth, and protected them from strangers. Within a few days of Kannah taking over, the two kittens finally eliminated and were soon back to their playful kittenlike antics of rolling in the grass and chasing small bugs. Not only did Kannah save the lives of the two constipated kittens, she also gave the entire litter the affection and physical contact they missed from their natural mom. Cathy believes that humans could learn a lot from the selfless behavior Kannah displayed.

Be the Hero of Your Own Life

HEROISM TAKES many forms. Sometimes it's an overt action for which the person is hoping for fame or money; but more often the most profound heroic acts are the ones done covertly—the ones where the hero acts instinctively and modestly. Our animal friends epitomize the actions of a humble hero, and through their example, we can learn how to incorporate heroism into our own lives every day.

Heroism is not merely acting courageous when the time arises. It's also stepping up to the plate and doing good for others without having to be asked. It's recognizing our talents and using them to help others. A heroic act can be as drastic as saving someone from a fire, as Muffin did, or as subtle as providing for a basic need, as Kannah did. The lesson is to learn to recognize these moments when they occur within us, then to trust our instincts to do the right thing.

When you become a hero in your own life, you gain a greater sense of awareness and respect for yourself and for those around you. You also become more aligned with your values and are willing to stand up for them when needed. As a result of staying true to your beliefs and helping others in need, you begin to see all the gifts you can offer the world while you recognize the talents others bring to the mix. Those who are heroes in their own lives discover that we can use our individual talents to better the world as a whole.

Being a humble hero is a necessary part of the human experience. Let us learn from all the examples our animal friends give us every day so we can make heroism an inspirational and vital part of our character and our lives.

PET LESSON #8:

BEING A HUMBLE HERO

Exercises: How to Use This Pet Lesson in Your Everyday Life

1. Think of a hero in your own life. What did the person do? What is it about the person's presence that makes you feel as if he or she is heroic? What can you do to be more like this person?

2. Think about the next courageous step you need to take in your life. What is it specifically? What are the obstacles that are keeping you from taking it? What are some of the steps you can take to overcome them?

3. Take time to define the values by which you want to live your life. What do you stand for? Make a list of the guiding principles that are important to you. Now pick those that you are willing to sacrifice for.

4. Muffin's instincts told her what to do. What are your instincts telling you about a situation? Take time to stop what you are doing and "be" for a period of time. Are you living your life on automatic pilot? How can you stay attuned to what you instinctively know is right for you?

5. The next time you get a "gut feeling," stop and listen to it. What is it telling you to do? Why do you want to listen to it or ignore it? Is the "gut feeling" in alignment with your values? If so, what's stopping you from carrying it out?

6. Has an animal ever saved you from harm? What did you learn from the experience? Have you repaid that act of heroism by being the hero for someone else? If not, why?

7. Heroism is something we can teach others, and one simple act can have lifelong results. What can you do to teach people how to be a hero in their own lives?

CONCLUSION

I RECENTLY SPOKE with a woman who mentioned that she gets a lot of compliments on how loving and kind her children grew up to be. When I asked her why she thought that was, she immediately stated that they all grew up with animals. "It was the love and caring that my children shared with our cats, dogs, and birds that made them more sensitive to others," she said. "Some of my friends never liked my saying that because they didn't want to be bothered with the obligations of a pet. Some of them are real sorry now."

Surrounding our children with companion animals is a great jumping-off point for teaching a life of compassion and empathy, but it's not enough. We also need to take the time to show young people how to touch, hold, and attend to animals. We need to talk with them about their relationships with other living beings. And learning compassion and empathy isn't the only benefit of having a relationship with a companion animal. These relationships can help us learn many life lessons.

The lessons that animals teach are around us every day. They can be found in the wet kisses our dogs give us when we need them most, in our cats' tender purrs during a time of

187

nuzzling, and even in the unstoppable spirit of our hamsters and gerbils as they run in their wheels. The love they apparently have for life, for each other, and for their human companions inspires us to live our lives to the fullest and to embrace the wisdom that's inherent in every living creature.

When we open our hearts and accept what our companion animals have to teach us, we can gain not only the secrets to a more fulfilled life but also a greater sense of peace and compassion. As we learn to love others unconditionally, be emotionally available during times of need, act heroically in everyday situations, and find the joy in simple play, we raise our own consciousness to the world around us. What better gifts can we give our young?

The future rests in the hands of our children. Teaching them to respect all living creatures has ramifications far beyond the current generation. As Gandhi once said, "The greatness of a nation and its moral progress can be judged by the way its animals are treated." Let us fully prepare our children for both the challenges and the joys of adulthood by giving them all the necessary life skills to enable them to achieve a greater purpose for themselves and our world.

From now on, as you go about your day, think about this: What can you learn from an animal today that will make our world a better place tomorrow? And how can you share that with others? The lessons you will learn are indeed valuable— use them to make a difference in the lives of all living creatures.

Mary Hessler-Key, Ph.D., delivers keynote presentations, retreats, and workshops on What Animals Teach Us. For more information please visit: maryhesslerkey.com or call 813-831-9500.

REFERENCES

Chapter 1

1. American Pet Products Manufacturers Association. *Pet Owner's Manual.* www.appma.org.
2. Beil, Laura. "The Power of Pets." *Dallas Morning News,* 28 Dec. 1998.
3. Kundera, Milan. *The Unbearable Lightness of Being.* New York: HarperCollins, 1987.
4. Schoen, Allen. *Kindred Spirits: How the Remarkable Bond Between Humans and Animals Can Change the Way We Live.* New York: Broadway Books, 2001.
5. Serpell, James. *In the Company of Animals.* New York: Basil Blackwell, 1986.
6. See number 5 above.
7. Ryan, Ellen. "Survey on Pet Ownership." *Psychology Today,* July 1984.
8. See number 5 above.
9. See number 5 above.

Chapter 2

1. Stanton, Glenn T. *Why Marriage Matters: Reasons to Believe in Marriage in Post-Modern Society.* New York: Pinon Press, 1997.
2. See number one above.
3. See number one above.
4. Schoen, Allen. *Kindred Spirits: How the Remarkable Bond Between Humans and Animals Can Change the Way We Live.* New York: Broadway Books, 2001.
5. Bowen, Murray. *Family Therapy in Clinical Practice.* New York: Jason Aronson, 1978.
6. See number 4 above.
7. Harris, Catherine T. "Human-Pet Relationships Among Veterinary Clients." *Veterinary Technician* 9, no. 8 (1988): 424–30.
8. Topal, Jozsef, Adam Miklosi, Vilmos Csanyi, and Antal Doka. "Attachment Behavior in Dogs: A New Application of Ainsworth's Strange Situations Test." *Journal of Comparative Psychology* 112, no. 3 (1998): 219–29.
9. Hart, Lynette A., R. Lee Zasloff, Sandy Bryson, and Sara L. Christensen. "The Role of Dogs in Police Work and as Companions." Center for Animals in Society, School of Veterinary Medicine, University of California, Davis, 1997.
10. Beck, Alan, Aaron Honori Katcher, and Elizabeth Marshall Thomas. *Between Pets and People: The Importance of Animal Companionship.* New York: G. T. Putnam's Sons, 1983.
11. Neiburg, H., and A. Fischer. *Pet Loss.* New York: Harper and Row, 1982.

Chapter 3

1. Robin, Michael, and Robert ten Bensel. "Pets and the Socialization of Children." In *Universal Kinship: The Bond*

Between All Living Things. Edited by The Latham Foundation, R & E Publishing, Saratoga, CA, 1991. 174–96.

2. NIH Technology Assessment Workshop. *Health Benefits of Pets: Summary of Working Group.* Washington, D.C.: U.S. Department of Health and Human Services, 1988.

3. Levinson, Boris Mayer. *Pets and Human Development.* Springfield, Illinois: Charles C. Thomas, 1972.

4. Levinson, Boris Mayer. "Pets, Child Development, and Mental Illness." *Journal of the American Veterinary Medical Association,* 1970, 157: 1759–1766.

5. See number one above.

6. Beck, Alan, and Aaron Honori Katcher, and Elizabeth Marshall Thomas. *Between Pets and People: The Importance of Animal Companionship.* New York: G. T. Putnam's Sons, 1983.

7. Cain, Ann Ottney. "Pets as Family Members." *Marriage and Family Review* 8, no. 3 (1985): 6.

8. See number one above.

9. See number one above.

10. Melson, G. F. "The Role of Companion Animals in Human Development." Paper presented at the Seventh International Conference on Human-Animal Interactions, Geneva, Switzerland, September 6–9, 1995.

11. Harvey, Ashley, Carolyn Butler, and Laurel Lagoni. "Children and Pet Loss, Part 1." *Veterinary Technician* 20, no. 5 (1999): 283–85.

12. See number one above.

13. See number eleven above.

14. See number one above.

15. See number eleven above.

16. See number six above.

17. Endenburg, Nienke, and Ben Baarda. "The Role of Pets in Enhancing Human Well-Being: Effects on Child Development." *The Waltham Book of Human-Animal Interactions: Benefits and Responsibilities.* Oxford: Pergamon Press, 1995: 7–18.

18. See number ten above.

19. Poresky, Robert H. "Companion Animals and Other Factors Affecting Young Children's Development." *Anthrozoos* 9, no. 4 (2000): 159–68.

Chapter 4

1. "Instinct." In Microsoft Encarta Online Encyclopedia 2001. http://encarta.msn.com. 1997–2001 Microsoft Corporation.

2. Goleman, Daniel. *Emotional Intelligence.* New York: Bantam Books, 1995.

3. Goleman, Daniel. "Leadership That Gets Results." *Harvard Business Review,* March–April 2000, 78–90.

Chapter 5

1. Schoen, Allen. *Kindred Spirits: How the Remarkable Bond Between Humans and Animals Can Change the Way We Live.* New York: Broadway Books, 2001.

2. Carkhuff, Robert R., and Bernard G. Berensen. *Beyond Counseling and Psychotherapy.* New York: Holt, Rinehart and Winston, 1967; reprint, 1977.

3. Rogers, C. R. "The Necessary and Sufficient Conditions of Therapeutic Personality Change." *Journal of Counseling Psychology* 22 (1957): 90–103.

4. Baun, M. M., N. Bergstrom, N. F. Langston, and L. Thoma. "Physiological Effects of Human/Companion Animal Bonding." *Nursing Research* 33, no. 3 (1984): 126–29.

5. See number four above.

6. Friedman, Erika, Aaron Honori Katcher, James J. Lynch, and Sue Anne Thomas. "Animal Companions and One-Year Survival of Patients After Discharge from a Coronary Care Unit." *Public Health Reports* 95, no. 4 (1980): 307–12.

7. See number one above.

8. Beil, Laura. "The Power of Pets." *Dallas Morning News*, 28 Dec. 1998.

9. See number one above.

10. Serpell, James. *In the Company of Animals.* New York: Basil Blackwell, 1986.

11. Hoffman, Rosemary G. "Companion Animals: A Therapeutic Measure for Elderly Patients." *Journal of Gerontology Social Work* 18, no. 1 (1991): 195–205.

12. House, J., C. Robbins, and H. Metzner. "The Association of Social Relationships and Activities with Mortality." *Tecumseh Community Health Study American Journal of Epidemiology* 116 (1982): 123–40.

13. Katcher, Aaron Honori. "People and Companion Animal Dialogue: Style and Physiological Response." *National Forum* 66, no. 1 (1986): 7–10.

14. Robin, Michael, and Robert ten Bensel. "Pets and the Socialization of Children." In *Universal Kinship: The Bond Between All Living Things.* 1991. 174–96. Edited by The Latham Foundation, R & E Publishing, Saratoga, CA.

Chapter 6

1. Van Praagh, James. *Healing Grief: Reclaiming Life After Any Loss.* New York: Dutton, Penguin Group, 2000.

2. National Hospice Organization. *Going Through Bereavement—When a Loved One Dies.* Pamphlet 713529, 1996.

3. National Hospice Organization. *Hospice Council of Metropolitan Washington.* Pamphlet 713461, 1996.

4. James, John W., and Frank Cherry. *The Grief Recovery Handbook.* New York: Harper and Row, 1988.

5. Allen, Karen. "Coping with Life Changes and Transitions: The Role of Pets." *Interactions* 13, no. 3 (1995): 5–6, 8–10.

6. Sable, Pat. "Pets, Attachment and Well-Being Across the Life Cycles." *Social Work* 40, no. 3 (1995): 334–38.

7. Rosenkoetter, Marlene M. "Health Promotion: The Influence of Pets on Life Patterns in the Home." *Holistic Nursing Practice* 5, no. 2 (1991): 42–51.

8. Garcia, Eddie. "Dealing with Pet Loss and Client Grief." *Norden News,* summer 1986, 5–10.

9. Bloom, Mary A. "When the Bond Is Broken: Companion Animal Death and Adult Human Grief." *The Lantham Letter,* winter 1986/87, 6–8.

Chapter 7

1. Bekoff, Marc, and John A. Byers, eds. *Animal Play: Evolutionary, Comparative, and Ecological Approaches.* Cambridge: Cambridge University Press, 1998.

2. Langer, Ellen J. and Mihnea Moldoveanu. "The Construct of Mindfulness." *Journal of Social Issues* 56, no. 1 (2000): 1–9.

3. White, Joanna, and Christopher T. Allers. "Play Therapy with Abused Children: A Review of the Literature." *Journal of Counseling and Development* 72, no. 4 (March 1994): 390-394.

4. Bekoff, Marc. "Animal Play: Lessons in Cooperation, Fairness, Spirit, and Soul." Unpublished, 2001.

5. Siviy, Stephen M. "Neurobiological Substrates of Play Behavior: Glimpses into the Structure and Function of Mammalian Playfulness." In Marc Bekoff and John A. Byers, eds., *Animal Play: Evolutionary, Comparative, and Ecological Approaches.* New York: Cambridge University Press, 1998: 221–242.

6. Tulku, Tarthang. *Skillful Means: Gentle Ways to Successful Work.* Berkeley, Calif.: Dharma Publishing, 1978.

7. Jackson, Phil. *Sacred Hoops: Spiritual Lessons of a Hardwood Warrior.* New York: Hyperion, 1995.

8. Langer, Ellen J. *Mindfulness.* New York: Addison-Wesley, 1989.

9. Bekoff, Marc. "The Essential Joys of Play." BBC Wildlife, August 2000: 46–53.
10. Thompson, Katrina V. "Self-Assessment in Juvenile Play." In Marc Bekoff and John A. Byers, eds., *Animal Play: Evolutionary, Comparative, and Ecological Approaches.* New York: Cambridge University Press, 1998: 183–204.
11. Spinka, Marek, Ruth C. Newberry, and Marc Bekoff. "Mammalian Play: Training for the Unexpected." *Quarterly Review of Biology* 76, no. 2 (2001): 141–68.
12. See number 11 above.

Chapter 8

1. Rachman, Stanley. *Fear and Courage* (2nd ed.). New York: W. H. Freeman, 1990.
2. Mott, MaryAnn. "Heart Smart." *Your Dog,* April 2000, 18–19.
3. Robin, Michael, and Robert ten Bensel. "Pets and the Socialization of Children." In *Universal Kinship: The Bond Between All Living Things.* 1991. 174–96. Edited by The Latham Foundation, R & E Publishing, Saratoga, CA.
4. Delta Society. *Benefits of a Service Animal/Service Dog.* Fact sheet, 2001.

INDEX